"As we begin to slowly transition into a new normal, some of us are recovering from illness or loss, and many of us are struggling with a loss of focus in our lives. If you are one of those who are not only looking forward to a new normal but also a new reason for being, I want to introduce you to Mark Scandrette and his new book *The Ninefold Path of Jesus*. If you're looking for a follower of Jesus who can offer you a pathway to a more compelling whole-life faith for times like these, check out this book. Mark will show you creative new ways to both be a difference and make a difference that reflect the ways of Jesus."

Tom Sine, coauthor with Dwight J Friesen of *2020s Foresight: Three Vital Practices for Thriving in a Decade of Accelerating Change*

"God has created a world where systems work in constant concert within systems, that in turn serve other systems. And God designed these nested systems to foster a profound sense of thriving. Yet we find ourselves functioning in systems that work against systems. And many of these systems—whether physiological, economic, ecological, or ethical—are woefully out of whack. Creating disjointed and dissonant rhythms, we march to toward our own demise. My dear friend Mark Scandrette has discerned a pathway of recovery in the ancient teachings of Jesus. Mark has distilled for us a practical, accessible, and joy-filled new way of showing up in our lives that restores harmony in the systems we are a part of through Jesus' Beatitudes. If you, like me, are wearing a weighted weariness brought on by old ways of thinking and being, *The Ninefold Path of Jesus* is the book for you."

Eric Leroy Wilson, poet and pastor of University Church of Christ, Malibu

"Mark continues his embodied spiritual formation in *The Ninefold Path of Jesus*. This book is a refreshing, embodied, honest, at-times-funny, at-times-emotionally moving exploration into following the way of Jesus. As a visual person, I appreciate the ways *The Ninefold Path of Jesus* aesthetically moves the reader from a passive to an engaged posture of formation. This book is a helpful resource for anyone seeking to continue to walk fully, one step after the other, with Jesus and with others."

Noemi Vega Quiñones, InterVarsity's LaFe ministry, coauthor of *Hermanas: Deepening Our Identity and Growing Our Influence*

"'It overwhelmed me. . . . He had such talent, he could find things inside a song and vigorously develop them,' was Bob Dylan's response to hearing Jimi Hendrix's rendition of 'All Along the Watchtower.' When encountering Mark's material on the Beatitudes, that's the quote that came to mind. I've played, taught, and sought to live these teachings for two decades, but wow! Watch how Mark can play it!"

Jarrod McKenna, founding CEO of CommonGrace.org.au and an Extinction Rebellion organizer

"*The Ninefold Path of Jesus* offers accessible yet penetrating insights into the transformative power of these core Christian teachings, which are often misunderstood and more often avoided. This is not just a book to be read, it is a book to be done. Holistic participation in Scripture is applied to contemporary challenges at once personal and social, with signposts for new consciousness along the way. Scandrette's approach is courageous, real, and raw, and opens space for the blessings of Jesus in similar fashion."

Adam A. Ghali, associate professor of marriage and family therapy at Fresno Pacific Biblical Seminary

"Mark Scandrette is a poet, an artist, and an instigator of holy mischief. In this book, he explores the wisdom of the Beatitudes of Jesus. If you set out to compile a list of values that contradict the highest aspirations of popular American culture, you couldn't do much better than the Beatitudes of Jesus, where Christ blesses the poor, the meek, the merciful, the peacemakers. In short, Jesus blesses all the people that our world is crushing, and he includes the people we have excluded. If you're not yet convinced that the call of Jesus is countercultural and revolutionary, just consider Christ's Beatitudes and Mark's reflections on them in this book. Jesus is literally flipping the world upside-down . . . or rightside up . . . so that the last are first and the first are last. This is what God is up to, and we are invited to be a part of it. Let Mark Scandrette lead you into the hidden secrets of Jesus. If we want to be blessed by God, we need to be near to the people that this world is crushing. The blessing is not at the top but at the bottom."

Shane Claiborne, author, activist, and cofounder of Red Letter Christians

"This book is important. Mark Scandrette wrests the Beatitudes out of the realm of sentimentality and theoretical abstraction. He dares to propose that Jesus meant what he said, and that what he said was meant to change everything. Jesus' invitation into the Beatitude life is not a nice-sounding series of phrases but something for us to receive and to practice. Scandrette gives us a sound curriculum to posture ourselves away from the world's fear, despair, self-centeredness, and apathy, and to posture ourselves toward Jesus' offer of trust, humility, lament, justice, compassion, peacemaking, surrender, and radical love. Following in this way seems to be our best hope for living a life that is free, hopeful, and blessed."

Aaron White, co-national director of 24-7 Prayer Canada and author of *Recovering: From Brokenness and Addiction to Blessedness and Community*

"Mark Scandrette issues us a compelling and winsome invitation to cultivate the kingdom of God within and around us, and then hands us tools so we can roll up our sleeves and dig in. Poet and activist, both grounded and visionary, he is a master craftsman in spiritual formation. This book will inspire and equip you to emulate both the radical heart orientation and lifestyle of Jesus."

Jill Weber, 24-7 Prayer International leadership team and author of *Even the Sparrow: A Pilgrim's Guide to Prayer, Trust and Following the Leader*

"As a fellow student of the Beatitudes, I've loved getting to know Mark Scandrette in the past year. Our mutual passion has inspired conversations that have taught me so much and, beyond just talking, have helped me live differently in the world. I think the Beatitudes show us where God is and invite us to live in a different kind of way. This book is Jesus' extended invitation to us to know and practice this Jesus way. I have heard that the goal of Christian maturity is not independence but interdependence. Mark's questions and practices in this book guide us to a life of interdependence—dependence on divine presence and on our need for each other. We are not alone on the hill. I will be recommending *The Ninefold Path of Jesus* to everyone I know and letting the content challenge me and change me for many years to come."

Stu Garrand, curator of The Beatitudes Project, former guitarist with Delirious?

"In *The Ninefold Path of Jesus*, Mark Scandrette provides an innovative and fresh approach to the Beatitudes, provocatively asserting that they 'point us toward what is real and true.' Scandrette's very practical and engaging interpretation of the Beatitudes, with exercises to lead us forward, makes this a valuable book for Christian leaders and discipleship programs."

Christine Sine, author of *The Gift of Wonder: Creative Practices for Delighting in God*

"Mark's use of the Beatitudes is a brilliant approach to discipleship. The idea of using Jesus' posture within these nine principles works equally well to light a spark in a stale religious rhythm as it does to lay a path for the spiritually curious. Whether you're looking to craft a new discipleship system for your church, rethink the way you talk about your faith, or transform your own spiritual development, looking at the Beatitudes through Mark's lens provides a typical-of-Jesus counterintuitive means to each end."

Angela Lam, pastor in Petaluma, California, and partner liaison for JesusCollective.com

"We're neck high in dogma and pink tea discussions about the correct parsing of Greek verbs. The question on the table is, What do the teachings of Jesus have to say to a bruised world in search of healers? Follow Mark Scandrette as he leads you through *The Ninefold Path of Jesus*. Next, follow his example. Take these teachings outside, far beyond your comfort zone. The world will be rewarded, and so will you."

Harry Louis Williams, ordained minister and author of *Taking It to the Streets: Lessons from a Life of Urban Ministry*

The Ninefold Path of Jesus

Hidden Wisdom of the Beatitudes

Mark Scandrette

An imprint of InterVarsity Press
Downers Grove, Illinois

InterVarsity Press
P.O. Box 1400, Downers Grove, IL 60515-1426
ivpress.com
email@ivpress.com

InterVarsity Press® is the book-publishing division of InterVarsity Christian
Fellowship/USA®, a movement of students and faculty active on campus at hundreds
of universities, colleges, and schools of nursing in the United States of America, and
a member movement of the International Fellowship of Evangelical Students. For
information about local and regional activities, visit intervarsity.org.

All Scripture quotations, unless otherwise indicated, are taken from The Holy Bible,
New International Version®, NIV®. Copyright © 1973, 1978, 1984, 2011 by Biblica,
Inc.™ Used by permission of Zondervan. All rights reserved worldwide.
www.zondervan.com. The "NIV" and "New International Version" are trademarks
registered in the United States Patent and Trademark Office by Biblica, Inc.™

While any stories in this book are true, some names and identifying information may
have been changed to protect the privacy of individuals.

Portions of this book were previously published as The Ninefold Path Notebook
©2017 Lifewords and The Ninefold Path Learning Lab | Group Guide ©2018
Lifewords. Used by permission.

The publisher cannot verify the accuracy or functionality of website URLs used in this
book beyond the date of publication.

Illustrations created by Leah Sands (de Lange)

Cover design and image composite: David Fassett
Interior design: Daniel van Loon
Image: paper texture background: © Svetlanais / iStock / Getty Images Plus
Author photo by Eric Niequist

ISBN 978-0-8308-4684-9 (print)
ISBN 978-0-8308-4685-6 (digital)

Printed in the United States of America ♾

InterVarsity Press is committed to ecological stewardship and to the conservation of
natural resources in all our operations. This book was printed using sustainably
sourced paper.

Library of Congress Cataloging-in-Publication Data
A catalog record for this book is available from the Library of Congress.

P	20	19	18	17	16	15	14	13	12	11	10	9	8	7	6	5	4	3	2	1
Y	38	37	36	35	34	33	32	31	30	29	28	27	26	25	24	23	22	21

To Danielle Welch and Steve Bassett

*Thank you for inviting me into your
dream to see a new generation awaken to
the revolutionary way of the Beatitudes.
May it be so.*

Contents

Introduction

Nine Postures for Life

Shortly after my first book was published, a Zen priest contacted me. He wrote, "My name is Shinko. I believe you are the kind of Christian I could talk to about what is happening in my life."

Over dinner a few weeks later, he explained,

I came to Jesus during the seventies Jesus movement. The church I joined taught me that only groups like ours had the right beliefs and that everyone else is going to hell. That didn't sit well with me, and I became disaffected with the church as I knew it then. I began exploring Judaism and Eastern philosophy. Eventually, I became a dedicated student of Zen Buddhism. I have lived and worked at Green Gulch monastery for the past fifteen years.

What I'm trying to make sense of is . . . when I practice sitting meditation (*zazen*), I hear Jesus calling to me—and I don't know what to do with that.

I asked Shinko what he believed about Jesus. He paused thoughtfully and replied, "I *adore* Jesus." Tears began streaming down his cheeks. "I don't know if I'd be considered orthodox by many Christians. But in my heart I know that I *adore* Jesus."

Shinko and I became fast friends. We were an odd pair walking the streets of my neighborhood, a young pastor and a cheerful shorn-headed priest wearing a *rakusu*, robe, and sandals. In restaurants and cafés people would stop and smile at Shinko and bow respectfully.

At the time I wasn't particularly conversant with faith traditions outside my own. So one day I asked Shinko, "What is the way of Zen Buddhism? When you wake up each day, what do you seek to do and be?"

In about four minutes Shinko succinctly answered my question. First, he named the Four Noble Truths. Then he explained the Eightfold Path: right understanding, right thought, right speech, right action, right livelihood, right effort, right mindfulness, and right concentration. "Each day I seek to deepen my experience of this path."

I was struck by how clear and concrete his answer was.

Then Shinko turned and asked me, "Mark, you identify as a follower of Jesus. When you wake up each day, what do you seek to do and be?"

I hesitated. My first impulse was to explain how I'd become a Christian. But that wasn't the question. I quickly recovered and said, "Each day I try to love God with my whole being and love my neighbor as myself."

I congratulated myself for giving an adequate answer. But I was haunted by how vague my response was compared to Shinko's. What, exactly, do I do each day to love God and people? I didn't have a clear answer.

How This Book Came to Be

On a summer evening in 2015 I was having drinks in a London pub with my friends Danielle and Steve. I asked Danielle about the most recent bombing in the city. She told me that ten young people a month are reportedly recruited and radicalized into terrorist organizations. "Meanwhile," she exclaimed, "church participation in the UK continues to plummet. We simply aren't giving young people a compelling vision for life!"

I mentioned what was happening back home in the United States. A series of highly publicized police shootings had galvanized the newly minted Black Lives Matter movement. In San Francisco, where I live, I'd recently been to the funeral of my twenty-year-old neighbor who had been shot six times in the back by two undercover officers.

Steve said, "It's clear that our systems are broken."

"And we are that system," I added. "What we need is a whole new way of being."

Steve and Danielle worked for a historic British Bible agency. With the prevalence of smartphones and Scripture apps, fewer people need printed Bibles anymore. "What does seems scarce," Steve said, "is a meaningful connection between Scripture and everyday life. Young people today have little interest in church, but that doesn't mean they aren't spiritually curious. Many would resonate with themes found in the Beatitudes—justice, peacemaking, nonviolence, etc."

"Has there ever been a moment when we've needed the message of the Beatitudes more?" Danielle exclaimed.

That night, Danielle and Steve invited me to join a project based on the Beatitudes called NINE BEATS Collective. My life passion is helping people apply the teachings of Christ to everyday life. So immediately I said yes.

I told Danielle and Steve that the project made me think of the haunting conversation I'd had with Shinko years before.

Danielle could see where the story was going. "So are you suggesting that the Beatitudes might be like the ninefold path of Jesus?" She asked.

"Exactly," I said. Dallas Willard used to say that the Sermon on the Mount is the best example we have of a "curriculum for Christlikeness." The problem is that there are one hundred ten verses in those three chapters. If most of us find it hard to remember a ten-digit phone number, no wonder we struggle to keep the teachings of Christ at the forefront of our minds. Maybe the Beatitudes can function as a thematic guide to the teachings of Christ.

I grabbed a napkin and Danielle handed me a pen, and we began to brainstorm. *Blessed are the poor.* That seems like an invitation to the way of trust. *Blessed are those who mourn.* That sounds like an invitation to lament what's broken in our world and inside of us. *Blessed are the meek*—that's an invitation to the way of humility. By the time we'd finished our drinks, we had a tentative sketch of the ninefold path of Jesus, inspired by the Beatitudes.

Over the next year we gathered artists, musicians, scholars, and activists from three continents to explore the wisdom of the Beatitudes together. We made a commitment to be ruthlessly honest. We examined how the Beatitudes challenge the dominant systems of society and our typical responses to life. We took on practices and experiments to help us understand the new consciousness the Beatitudes point us to. Eventually, we published two resources: *The Ninefold Path Learning Lab* and *The Ninefold Path Notebook.* Over the last five years I've traveled to five continents and invited thousands of people to explore the radical invitation of the Beatitudes. And with this book, I'm inviting you to join us.

What Are the Beatitudes?

The teachings on the hill found in the Gospel of Matthew are the fullest record we have of what Jesus regularly taught as he traveled throughout Galilee. It begins with nine strange blessings traditionally called the Beatitudes. *Makarios* is the Greek word Jesus uses, which means something like "incredibly fortunate, favored, or Godlike." It's a term we might use to describe the most privileged and admired star athlete, celebrity, or billionaire. Jesus begins by saying:

> Blessed (or Godlike) are
> the poor,
> those who mourn,
> the meek,
> those hungry for justice,
> the merciful,
> the pure in heart,
> the peacemakers,
> the persecuted
> and blessed are you . . .

Imagine Jesus making these statements as he walks through a crowd, putting his hand on the shoulder of a beggar as he says, "Blessed are the poor," locking eyes with a grieving widow as he says, "Blessed are those who mourn," or lifting the chin of a peasant laborer as he says, "Blessed are the meek."

What's surprising is who Jesus calls fortunate. At the time, people assumed that only the most wealthy, attractive, or powerful were blessed. Poor, sad, and suffering people were thought to be cursed. Still today it can feel like our circumstances, identity, or previous choices exclude us from the blessed life. With these strange blessings Jesus announces that a thriving life, under God's care, is available to anyone. Whatever your story, whatever your struggle, wherever you find yourself, this path is available to you.

If we look only at the first three Beatitudes, it might seem like the whole point is that a blessed life is available to unlikely people. But the next four Beatitudes celebrate noble qualities: a hunger for justice, mercy, purity of heart, and peacemaking. This shift suggests that Jesus is introducing a more comprehensive picture of what the blessed life looks like and how to experience it.

Nine Shifts in Consciousness

The Beatitudes name nine distinct areas of human struggle that Jesus addresses in his teaching on the hill. Our first instincts are to be anxious, avoidant, competitive, apathetic, judgmental, evasive, divided, retaliatory, and afraid. Several of these instincts are related to mental health issues. If you are experiencing clinical anxiety, post-traumatic stress, depression, paranoid thinking, or other conditions, please seek professional help. Neurological research suggests that many of these patterns of perception are wired into the biology of our brains. For example, to keep us alive, the fight-or-flight response alerts us to potential dangers. But to thrive we must learn to move from anxiety to trust: "Blessed are the poor in spirit." Similarly, racism is built into our biology. We instinctually distrust people who have different skin tones and facial features than we do. To thrive we must reach past these differences: "Blessed are the peacemakers."

First instincts explain a lot about the conditions we see in the world. Anxiety about having enough is the cause of so much striving and greed, and the growing gap between the rich and the poor. Our tendency to avoid pain produces a distracted and entertainment-addicted culture and the inability of those with the power to take responsibility for the harm they cause. Our competitive instincts are responsible for our obsession with achievement and success. Our learned helplessness has led us to believe that we can do little to address systemic injustices. Our tendency toward judgment and contempt produces conflict and division. Our impulse toward shame makes us image-conscious, distrustful, and alienated from others. Our instinct toward dualistic us-versus-them thinking creates tension and division in public and private life. Our tendency to retaliate leads to preemptive wars and a punitive correctional system. Our fear of death leads us to choose self-preservation over courage and self-giving love.

First instincts are necessary for our early survival, but they eventually become toxic. To thrive we must transcend our automatic responses and learn to see and act from a more complete and accurate understanding of reality. Jesus claimed that he understood the true nature of reality, which he called "the kingdom of God." His invitation was to rethink or reimagine our whole lives—to see in a new way. His teachings challenge many of our instinctual ways of seeing, with the signature phrase, "You have heard that it was said, *but* I tell you . . ."

In this book I'm using the Beatitudes to represent nine shifts we are invited to make in order to live in greater coherence with reality. To live in a new way and to see the world become different and better, we must learn to act from this higher state of kingdom consciousness. Jesus invites us to confront our distorted responses to life and return to what is most real and true. The Beatitudes chart this path back to reality.

The Beatitudes name the illusions and false beliefs that have kept us chained and imprisoned. We've learned to live from a mentality of anxiety and greed, but what if this is a world of abundance? We've learned to live as if there is no option but despair, but what if solace and comfort are near? We've learned to live by striving, competing, and comparing, but what if we all have equal dignity and worth?

The Beatitudes point us toward what is real and true. We are not helpless. We have the power to do good and seek justice. Mercy triumphs over judgment. We can stop hiding and pretending, and be honest.

The Beatitudes invite us to a new way of life, into a path of recovery. Instead of dividing the world into us and them, we can learn to embrace each other as family. Instead of resisting pain, we can learn to be resilient and join the cosmic struggle between good and evil. Instead of living in fear, we can choose hope, courage, and radical love.

Big ideas like trust, compassion, and peacemaking can easily become abstractions. How can we explore these themes in a more personal and tangible way? We integrate what we learn more fully when we engage our whole bodies and reflect on our lived experiences. For each Beatitude I introduce a physical position, or stance, that illustrates the first instinct. Then I invite you to consider a new posture that embodies the invitation to see and live in a new way. Because we learn kinesthetically, engaging your mind, body, and emotions together will help you remember and internalize each step along the ninefold path.

Honesty is an important beginning point for the journey of growth. In this book I will identify where I struggle to live in the higher consciousness the Beatitudes point us to. I'm inviting you to explore how these nine invitations speak to circumstances in your life. Personality, culture, and life experience shape the landscape of our journeys. As you read through descriptions of the ninefold path, you may want to consider which Beatitude realities you find easier or more difficult to embrace.

Each chapter includes animating questions that you may wish to pause to reflect on and journal about. Suggested practices will be introduced that you can try immediately. I will also share stories about experiments and practices that have helped me and others live in a new way. You may want to read and talk through this book with a friend or group of friends and try the suggested practices together.

I am grateful to have spent the past five years immersed in the hidden wisdom of the Beatitudes. I don't feel like I am anywhere close to mastering the life they point us toward. But I do feel like I now have a better answer to the question Shinko asked me, "When you wake up each morning, what do you seek to do and be?"

1

The Way of Trust

Own Your Poverty, Live with Open Hands

*Blessed are the poor in spirit, for
theirs is the kingdom of heaven.*

MATTHEW 5:3

We greet the world with a cry and a scream, with clinched fists grasping after what we so desperately need. None of us remember the shock and drama of being born, but have you seen a baby's birth? I vividly recall the moment when my wife, Lisa, gave birth to our first child, Hailey. Hailey was warm and safe inside her mother's body. Everything she needed came through a tube into her belly. Then suddenly she was thrust into a cold, harsh world, naked, gasping for breath, and bombarded by bright lights and loud noises. Red-faced and crying, she squeezed her tiny fists in protest.

Our brains are wired to detect danger. Primal anxiety keeps us alive at birth. The fight-or-flight response activates the amygdala, increasing heart rate and blood-sugar levels, giving a temporary boost of energy to react. But when our brains become flooded with adrenaline, we can't think clearly, and it's hard to calm down. That's why a baby needs a caregiver's soothing voice and touch.

An anxious response can be activated even when there isn't imminent danger—by the sound of a car alarm or when a loved one is late and doesn't call. Our constant scanning for potential danger can result in hyperarousal and chronic stress. An instinct, designed to keep us alive, can quickly become a threat to well-being.

At the beginning of his teaching on the hill, Jesus said, "Blessed are the poor in Spirit, for theirs is the kingdom of heaven." Luke's account simply says, "Blessed are you who are poor." What does it mean to be poor? Poverty is when a person doesn't have enough or when they feel like they are not enough. Something is lacking materially or emotionally.

> **❓ What's your poverty? Where in your life do you feel like you don't have enough or are not enough?**

When I posed this question to a group in East Africa, one person said, "I don't have the fees to pay for my children's schooling." Another said, "My son was born without the ability to eliminate. The surgery costs three hundred dollars, but we don't have the money. And if he doesn't have the surgery soon, he will die!"

I am grateful not to be in this incredible predicament. But we each have places in our lives where something is lacking. Ultimately, none of us have enough. We each experience loss, loneliness, and disappointment. Eventually, we will all get sick or injured or grow old and die. While we each experience lack in our lives, those of us with control-oriented personalities feel particularly pained by our vulnerabilities. We act aggressively to ensure that we are never dependent, out of control, or lacking anything.

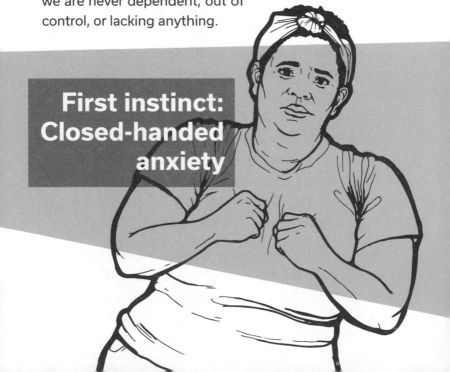

First instinct: Closed-handed anxiety

When we become aware of what we lack, our first instinct is to grab and grasp, holding on to whatever we believe will make us feel safe and secure. It's an instinct of closed-handed anxiety. Not letting go. Imagine closing your hands and squeezing until your knuckles are tight. How does that feel? Tense? Stiff? Uncomfortable? That's a position of anxiety, and it's the source of the worry, striving, and greed that pervade our world.

What makes you feel anxious and closed handed? I feel anxious when I think about political and economic uncertainties in our world today. I often worry about getting all the things done on my to-do list. Sometimes I worry about my children. Will they thrive, find good partners, and live the values I've taught them? I worry about having enough money to pay for expenses when I'm too old to work. But more than anything else, I worry about whether I'm competent and successful.

When I mention my work insecurities, people are quick to assure me that I am competent—yet it's still something I often feel anxious about. Our worries aren't always rational but feel very real to us.

PRACTICE *Confronting worry.* If you were to make a list of the top five things you tend to worry about, what would they be? Take a moment to make a mental list or write them down.

At Ninefold Path events I ask people to anonymously write their worries on sticky notes. We post them to a wall and look at them together. Participants are often surprised by the raw honesty of what is shared and the private burdens that people they know carry. Here are a few examples:

▸ I worry I'll never find love and that I'll die alone.

▸ I worry about having money to buy groceries for my family.

▸ I worry about whether people like me or just put up with me.

▸ I worry that I will never overcome my addiction.

▸ I worry that I am missing God's path for my life.

▸ I worry that I'll never get out of debt or own a home.

▸ I worry about the climate crisis and the future of the planet.

▸ I worry that I can't think of any worries. Am I in complete denial?

We don't all have the same worries, but there are predictable patterns to the kinds of things we tend to worry about: (1) money, job, and finances; (2) physical and mental health; (3) relationships and the well-being of those we love; (4) esteem, identity, and significance; and (5) anticipating future difficulties, pain, and uncertainty.

It is a sacred trust to hold each other's worries. Sharing your worries with another person can help you feel more normal and less alone. They can help you see your situation from a larger perspective.

In groups I often ask, "Why do you think we tend to worry?" Inevitably someone will say, "We worry about the things we can't predict or control." Another person often adds, "I think we worry because we care. How can we not care about the people we love and conditions in our world?"

It can help to clarify that worry and concern are not the same. When I'm concerned about something, it motivates me to action. If I'm alerted to the weight I've gained around my middle, I can take action by making new food and activity choices. If I'm concerned about a loved one's physical or mental health, I can provide support and assist them in exploring treatment options. In contrast, worry is a heightened state of alarm that changes nothing. The dreaded thought just loops on repeat. This is why Jesus said, "Who of you by worrying can add a single hour to your life?"

An anxious thought might wake you up at night, cause you to lose concentration, or distract you when you are spending time with someone. It zaps energy and paralyzes action. Worry even manifests in our bodies. Where do you hold it? In your stomach? Forehead? Chest? Neck and shoulders? Lower back?

Imagine being significantly free of worry and anxiety. What would that be like? Deep peace. Sound sleep. Full attention. Is that a quality of life you desire? Do you think it's possible?

In the teaching on the hill Jesus said, "Do not worry about your life." The apostle Paul echoed this when he wrote, "Do not be anxious about anything." When I hear the instruction "Do not worry," I'm tempted to feel shame because I do worry. But I'm learning to receive these instructions from Jesus as a gentle invitation into a better way. What would I have to see and believe differently about the nature of reality that would allow me to be less anxious?

Jesus knew by experience that it is possible to live in openhanded trust. He was once in a boat with his disciples when a terrible storm came up. They were completely freaked out while he napped in the back of the boat. He lived and practiced the reality of divine care and presence. The reality is that nothing can separate us from what is most essential to our well-being. Not disappointment. Not sickness. Not even death can separate us from the care and presence of our Creator. This is why the ancient poet King David once wrote, "[*Adonai*] is my shepherd, I lack nothing."

The Posture of Openhanded Trust

If you gently open your hands, how does it feel compared to clinched fists? Relaxed? Peaceful? Relieved? That's the posture of openhanded trust. When faced with the inevitable lack in our lives, we have a choice. We can follow instincts and close our hands in white-knuckled anxiety or open our hands in childlike trust.

Learning to Be Openhanded

What practices might help us move from closed-handed anxiety to openhanded trust?

Open your hands to receive the good. Have you ever gotten a new shirt and suddenly seen people wearing that color or print everywhere you turn? We notice what we pay attention to. Many of us are fatally attracted to bad news. When we

**New posture:
Openhanded trust**

focus on potential threats, we often miss the good. Fear and negativity are instinctual, but we can choose to be thankful. "Give thanks in all circumstances." Both ancient Scripture and contemporary psychology affirm the potency of gratitude.

PRACTICE *Gratitude.* Take a moment right now to open your hands to receive the good. What are you appreciating about this day and this moment? What can you see, hear, touch, taste, and smell right now that makes you feel alive and connected to what is good? When you look back over your life, where do you see evidence that you are cared for and loved?

Open your hands to share what you have. Anxiety breeds a sense of scarcity and greed. Gratitude fuels a sense of abundance, contentment, and generosity.

One time in northern Uganda a man approached me putting his hand to his mouth to gesture his hunger. Around the world hundreds of millions of people lack access to basic nutrition, health services, clean water, and public safety. Much of the inequality we see stems from greediness, corruption, waste, and the long-term effects of colonization. I'm curious to understand how my sisters and brothers in these places experience their lives. I have a friend from Uganda who now lives in the United States. When I asked him how he compares living in poverty with living in affluence he said, "I know I'm supposed to say I'm grateful to have a better life in the United States. But honestly, I feel lonely. In Kampala I was surrounded by friends and family. We didn't have much, but we had each other. We knew how to care for one another, and we made our own fun." Independence breeds a sense of scarcity. Poverty is not a blessing. But when you know you can't make it on your own, it may be easier to be openhanded and live interdependently.

We are meant to be part of the flow of abundance: to open our hands to receive what we need and share what we have with others. Jesus taught his followers to be radically generous when he said: "Sell your possessions and give to the poor" and then "They sold property and possessions to give to anyone who had need."

Inspired by this, I was once part of a group who challenged each other to sell or give away half of our possessions. Our experiment was deeply transforming. We decluttered our closets and homes. It exposed our unhealthy and consumptive spending patterns. We learned to be more content. And we experienced the joy of sharing resources with our neighbors in desperate circumstances around the world. "It is more blessed to give than to receive" is a truth proven by both research and experience. You can cultivate a posture of openhandedness by asking yourself each day, *What do I have that I can share with others? Time? Money? Or possessions and food that someone else can use?*

Open your hands to express your desires. When I am planning time with one of my children, I'll ask, "What do you want to do?" As moody teenagers they sometimes reply, "I don't know" or "I don't care." I love it when they know what they want and tell me, "Dad, can we get boba tea and go for a walk on the beach?" Relationships are strengthened when we have the courage to express our desires and seek to satisfy one another's needs.

I meet a lot of people who believe it's wrong to have desires. Or they hesitate to name their desires because they're afraid of being disappointed. One of the most compelling questions Jesus ever asked is, "What do you want me to do for you?" What if the Creator of the universe wants to have an interactive relationship with you in which you express your deepest longings? In the teaching on the hill Jesus invites us into this dynamic: "Ask and it will be given to you; seek and you will find; knock and the door will be opened to you. For everyone who asks receives; the one who seeks finds; and to the one who knocks, the door will be opened."

These words are sometimes taken to mean that all you have to do is ask, and if you have enough faith, you'll get whatever you want (health, wealth, prosperity). Has this been your experience? For most of us it hasn't, and it's led to a lot of disappointment. If we look at Jesus' words more carefully, he is telling us how to set our intentions and move toward the good in our lives. In order to ask, you have to know what you want. Sometimes I am half-hearted or conflicted about what I want. It's a step just to get in touch with your desires, pausing to ask, What do I want and why?

Asking is just the beginning. We need to put effort and discipline into it. Jesus invites us to seek and knock. What can you do today to move toward the good you desire? Investigate. Look for opportunities. Talk to the right people. Advocate for yourself. Keep knocking until a door opens that you want to walk through.

To some degree we all get what we want. Maybe not all we want but what we most deeply desire ends up finding its way to us. If you are skeptical about this, try writing down one desire each day for a month and see what happens.

Open your hands to let go of expectations. What might your worries reveal about your attachments? We may tell ourselves, *I can only be truly happy if I find a life partner, get my dream house or a particular job, or* _____. It's dangerous to make your sense of well-being contingent on a particular outcome. What if you don't get what you want? Or what if you do? You may get what you want only to discover that you are still unsatisfied. Clarifying true desire is part of the process. An object or outcome might be a symbol of what you truly long for. A car or clothing item might represent your desire to feel admired, respected, or worthy. A house might represent your desire for security and stability. A life partner might represent your desire for companionship. Career success might represent a deeper desire to feel purposeful and make a difference. Don't get stuck on specific outcomes. Focus on deeper longings. What do you want that you can actually experience today?

I know many people who struggle with faith or have lost faith because something in their life didn't go according to plan. They didn't get a particular job or into the school program they wanted. They had a miscarriage. An important relationship ended. Or a loved one died unexpectedly. Of course, these are difficult experiences, but they are also normal. I'm convinced that many of our prayers are recitations of our worries and attachments: *God, give me what I want or else!*

I have some bad news. Many of the things you worry about will come true. Ultimately, we don't get what we want. A time will come when all your accomplishments will be in the past. Some goals and dreams you have will never come to pass. Relationships you hoped would heal or become closer will reach an impasse. People you care about will leave you or pass away. And after all these losses and disappointments, you will get sick or injured and die. If our life satisfaction is contingent on always getting what we want, we are in big trouble!

Jesus invites us into radical trust: believing that nothing can separate us from what is most essential to our well-being. The divine presence is with us through whatever difficulties we face. It's an invitation to live with open hands, giving our sacred consent, and speaking a radical *yes!* to life, no matter what may come. It's an invitation to trust that the One who made us will bring us through.

When I'm struggling to move from anxiety to trust, I take a few deeps breaths, open my hands, and recite these words:

> Creator,
> my life is in you.
> I receive this moment as a gift.
> All that has been and what lies ahead remain a
> > mystery to me, kept hidden.
> But I trust in the love that spoke this world
> > into existence.
> I say yes to whatever this day may bring.
> Only let me see and cherish what is real.

How have you closed your hands? What are you holding on to? How does it feel to live this way?

Independence makes us feel we live in scarcity. We didn't make ourselves, and we don't have to make it on our own. We can learn to trust in the abundant provision of a good Creator. We are invited to open our hands, to live in gratitude, satisfaction, and generosity. To share what we have with one another and to see where that takes us.

This Beatitude invites us to move from closed-handed anxiety to openhanded trust: *Blessed are the poor in spirit, for theirs is the kingdom of heaven.*

May we own our poverty, celebrate the reality of abundance, live with open hands, and walk in the way of trust.

2

The Way of Lament

Face Your Pain, Wait for Comfort

Blessed are those who mourn,
for they will be comforted.

MATTHEW 5:4

No one likes to hear a baby cry. In buses, airplanes, and waiting rooms we do whatever we can to soothe and distract a sad child. We make funny faces, offer a snack, or pull out a phone to share a game or funny video. When you were small the adults in your life did whatever they could to comfort you. If you fell and scraped your hands and knees, someone likely scooped you up and said, "I know it hurts, but you'll be okay." As we got older we found our own ways to soothe ourselves and avoid pain.

Pain avoidance is a natural and largely unconscious survival strategy built into our biology. If you touch a hot stove, your hand will automatically pull away. Emotional injury also makes us recoil from people and situations that trigger us. Many children forget early trauma until the brain is more developed and it's safe to process. But the body remembers. In posttraumatic stress response, painful events are relived in an endless loop of unprocessed feelings, images, and physical sensations.

Our first instinct is to run from pain. We turn away, holding our hands up to block out whatever we find too difficult to face. That's the instinct of turning away from pain. We humans have always sought ways to escape, distract, or numb ourselves from the harsh realities of life.

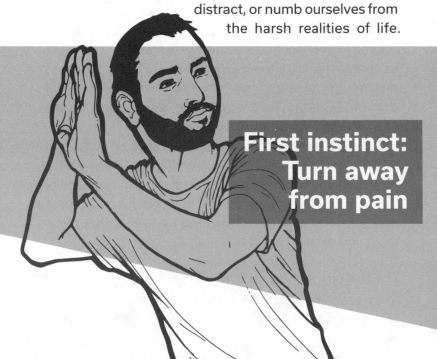

First instinct: Turn away from pain

While each of us tends to do this, some of us with personality traits sensitive to pain organize our whole lives around avoiding it at any cost. Never look back. Always focus on the future.

Maybe we run from pain because we think all that is there is despair. But as anyone in recovery knows, running from pain doesn't help. If your heart breaks and you don't take time to mourn, the pain only goes deeper. The sadness ends up leaking out in other ways: anger, stress, physical illness, depression, or dependency on food, entertainment, alcohol, drug use, or other compulsive activity. A friend once told me, "I have a lot of consumer debt because I shop to cope with the sexual trauma I experienced as a child." We can even use work to escape. Many of the things we use to escape weren't designed to provide lasting comfort. At the bottom of the bottle or when the binge-worthy series ends, we are still stuck with the same problems.

What if we could find another way? What if instead of running from our pain we could discover a truer and longer-lasting source of comfort? Imagine the possibility that you can experience solace at the point of deepest pain in your life. What would that be like? Is this something you desire?

The Posture of Facing Pain

In the teaching on the hill Jesus said, "Blessed are those who mourn, for they will be comforted." That's like saying,

"Happy are you when you are unhappy." With profound wisdom, Jesus invites us to stop running from our pain. He took time to mourn. When he heard that his cousin John had been beheaded, he withdrew by boat to a solitary place. When his friend Lazarus died, he wept bitterly at the grave (moments before bringing him back to life). He cried over the structural injustice of Jerusalem, where generations of prophets had been murdered. While being tortured and executed he refused to dull the pain with wine.

In ancient cultures, people knew how to mourn. They tore their clothes. They poured ashes on their heads. They sat in the dirt and raised their voices in lament. Imagine sitting on the ground, lowering your chin, and holding your head in your hands. That's the posture of facing pain.

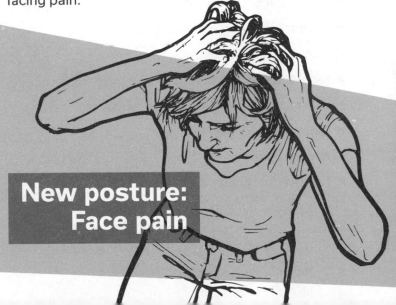

New posture: Face pain

PRACTICE *Mourning.* We live in a world of wonder and great beauty but also of difficulty and great tragedy. When you are mistreated, someone close to you dies, or you hear about the latest mass shooting, the only thing that makes sense is to grieve.

 When you look out at the world what breaks your heart? What do you see that makes you sad?

In our world there is so much to mourn:

▶ children separated from their parents in refugee camps

▶ the Covid-19 pandemic and growing income inequality

▶ starvation and extreme poverty

▶ violence and neglect in families

▶ sexual exploitation

▶ racial and gender prejudice and inequality

▶ mental illness, homelessness, and addiction

▶ loneliness and depression

▶ climate change

▶ current political divides

I feel sad about my daughter's chronic illness and disability, and the physical pain and loneliness she experiences. I feel sad about a strained relationship with someone I love. I feel regret about mistakes I've made as a spouse, parent, leader, and friend. When I look out the window, I grieve for my young neighbor who has schizophrenia, is unmedicated, and sleeps on the sidewalk. I try to help, but it's complicated.

> **?** **What about you? What's broken in you? Where do you feel loneliness, pain, disappointment, and loss?**

Grief is not a competition. Whatever causes your sadness needn't be compared with anyone else. "Each heart knows its own bitterness, and no one else can share its joy."

Why did Jesus invite us to face our pain? He had confidence in the divine presence to bring solace. Though you may feel alone, you are never alone. The divine presence is here to bring peace when nothing else makes sense. You can see this psychology in the ancient psalms:

> Why, my soul, are you downcast?
>   Why so disturbed within me?
> Put your hope in God,
>   for I will yet praise [God].

If we dare to name and sit with our pain, we may experience surprising comfort.

Learning to Sit with Pain and Wait for Comfort

What practices might help us move from avoiding to facing pain?

Face pain by making space to mourn. While visiting South Australia I went for a run before sunrise. A wild dog spooked me on the trail. I slipped and fell, badly scraping my knee. After cleaning away the blood I quickly put a bandage over it—it looked ugly. After several weeks the wound still oozed and throbbed and woke me up at night. *Why isn't it getting any better?* I wondered. The wound needed to breathe. I peeled off the bandage, and it finally began to heal.

The soul also needs space to breathe and time to mourn. Limiting or abstaining from our normal escapes can make that possible. Fasting is a traditionally recognized way to express grief. Jesus assumed that his followers would fast, and he encouraged them not to make a big deal of it.

What does fasting do? Let's say that one night at nine o'clock I am feeling a bit lonely and sad. I think, *Maybe some ice cream will help*. So I go to the freezer, scoop a few bites, or maybe even eat the whole pint. Temporarily, I feel better. A part of the brain called the basal ganglia memorizes this stimulus-response loop. The next time I feel sad, stressed, or lonely, I may reach for the ice cream without consciously thinking. My response becomes automatic. Fasting arrests this pattern. When I don't follow the script, my brain searches for a novel solution. What else can I do right now? Might there be a better way to process these sad feelings?

I was recently in a Ninefold Path group in which we each chose something to give up for a week to make space to mourn. One person chose social media. Another, sugary snacks. Another, alcohol. I chose to abstain from my screen habit. I don't think there is anything inherently wrong with enjoying television, but I'd become dependent on TV as a nightly escape. On the first evening I complained, "What am I going to do between now and bedtime!" I took a solitary walk, read on the couch, and went to bed early. Gradually, my fast led to moments of deeper reflection. It also made space for an important conversation with Lisa that hadn't occurred because I'd been numbing out.

What's the difference between avoiding pain and seeking appropriate comfort? I have a friend who says, "The first episode of my favorite TV show is soothing. But if I'm watching the fifth episode in a row, I know I've crossed the line into numbing." Another friend comments, "A glass of red wine at the end of a long day is comforting. But if I'm pouring my third or fourth glass, I've slid into escape." Soothing activities like a warm bath, a heartfelt talk with a friend, or a solitary walk don't usually become compulsive the way our escapes do. The difference between comfort and avoidance is, ultimately, something you will only know for yourself. *What are the things you most often go to for comfort and escape? What would you consider limiting or giving up for a time to make space to mourn?*

Face pain by waiting in stillness. Our energy and attention often go toward looking back with regret or looking forward with anxiety. Divine comfort is found in the present moment, where you are right now: "Be still, and know that I am God."

Julian of Norwich, a fourteenth-century mystic, experienced tremendous pain in her life. Her parents were both killed in the black plague. She suffered from chronic illness and nearly died in early in adulthood. Gradually, she discovered joy and peace amid her difficulties. This well-known quote is attributed to her: "All shall be well, and all shall be well, and all manner of things shall be well."

PRACTICE *Waiting in stillness.*

The only way to discover the potential comfort of divine presence is through direct experience. Try waiting in stillness now. Find a comfortable way to sit at attention. Focus on your breath. Breathe in deeply, then exhale slowly. Notice how your body feels as you continue to breathe in and out. Stay present in the moment. If you get distracted by thinking about the past or future, return to your breath. Some people are helped by focusing on a favorite name for God or a short breath prayer like "I have stilled and quieted my soul." Try waiting like this for the next five minutes. *Do you find it easy or difficult to still your mind and heart?*

Face pain by writing a complaint. Sometimes, when we sit in stillness, we feel comfort. But what about those times when we wait and feel nothing but despair? When we can't make sense of what we experience, we're invited to complain. An astonishing number of the ancient psalms were songs of lament or complaint:

> Awake, Lord! Why do you sleep?
>> Rouse yourself! . . .
> Why do you hide your face
>> and forget our misery and oppression?

Jesus quoted one of these psalms to express his anguish while being executed:

> My God, my God, why have you forsaken me?
>> Why are you so far from saving me,
>> so far from my cries of my anguish?

When you feel abandoned, you can write your own song, poem, or letter of complaint. Acknowledge the things that make you feel angry, sad, confused, or powerless. If you dare to express your disappointment to God you may be surprised by the comfort you experience.

I once led a Ninefold Path experience for a diverse group of younger and older people in Wales. Many of them had been pretty beaten up by life. One young person had so little self-regard that they had used a tattoo gun to doodle all over their body. When I asked about a triangle tattoo on the side of their shaved head, they said, "It was supposed to say, 'I am beloved' but I accidentally wrote it backward, so I scribbled over it."

I invited everyone to spend time in silence and solitude. If they felt like they needed to, they could write a complaint. Two hours later we regathered to read our poems. A young woman whose best friend had died of an opioid overdose went first. She said, "I realize that until today I hadn't given myself permission to grieve his death." A beefy middle-aged trade worker tearfully read a poem expressing regret about the kind of father he'd been to his daughter. Then an older women read a beautifully haunting piece about the sorrow she feels when she visits her husband in a care home. "He has Alzheimer's and doesn't recognize me anymore," she explained. One by one people shared in English and Welsh. By the end all seventy of us were in tears. It was cathartic to lament together and made us feel less alone and more seen and heard.

Face pain by mourning with those who mourn. Western culture is based on the pursuit of happiness. But does trying to be happy all the time make us happy? Many difficult things happen in life. Hearing someone tell us to "just cheer up" rarely helps. Our discomfort with pain can make it challenging to be present to others in their pain. We easily go into the problem-solving mode or share well-meaning platitudes that end up making the other person feel even more alone. We are invited to bear witness to other's pain without trying to fix it—to "mourn with those who mourn."

We may be uncomfortable with other people's sorrow because their pain implicates us or highlights the privileges we have in unequal systems. Those of us from ruling or majority groups often benefit directly or indirectly from the mistreatment of others. Instead of mourning with them, we may react defensively, denying, minimizing, or blaming them for their pain. If you find yourself having a strong critical reaction to someone else's expression of lament, it is worth exploring where that arises from. "The inability to mourn" is a term coined by German psychoanalyst Margarete Mitscherlich to explain this phenomenon, which she observed among Germans who were complicit in Nazi atrocities.

My friends of color have taught me a lot about the critical role of lament. A few years ago Lisa and I were invited to spend three days exploring the ninefold path with a group of young Aboriginal leaders in South Australia. We had the honor of being welcomed to the country by Robert, a young elder. In my acknowledgment of the country I thought it important to also pay respect to the original custodians of the land where I grew up, the Ojibwe Nation, and the unceded land where I now live that belonged to the Ramaytush Ohlone people.

"Better try some kangaroo tail before the children eat it all," Rhanee said. "We consider it a delicacy." She handed me a hot hairy chunk that had been roasted over the coals of a fire. I peeled the crispy skin and took a bite. It tasted unctuous, sweet, and gamey. The scent of the oily meat stayed on my hands for days.

Sean, a student, took me aside and showed me an Australian two-dollar coin. "That's a traditional Aboriginal man. He's just like me." He continued, "If you look at the other coins, you'll notice they all have animals on them—and that's what they thought of us—that we were animals. Even though we've lived on this land for sixty thousand years, we weren't considered fully human or given the right to vote until the referendum of 1967."

I asked Sean and Rhanee to teach me about lament. "Oh, we know all about mourning," Rhanee said. "So many of us are sick or dying. Every week we go to a hospital or a funeral." Rhanee herself has kidney disease, is on dialysis, and is awaiting a kidney transplant. "Genetically, our bodies are made to eat kangaroo and bush foods. The Western diet, including healthy greens, make us sick."

The next day Sean took us to a sacred site, a spring near the beach in Adelaide. It was littered with garbage from a nearby construction site. As we sat near the murky water, he told us an ancient story of lament. "Tjilbruke had two nephews he loved very much. The two boys fought and one killed the other. When Tjilbruke found out, he was overcome with grief. He walked this coast, stopping seven times to weep. The land also wept, producing this spring and six others. They continue to bear witness to his tears." We sat silently by the spring for an hour, reflecting on our own pain and the collective grief of Aboriginal peoples.

As the sun set over the sea, we watched Dusty Feet Mob dance, a troupe of women and girls who use their performances to create dialogue about Aboriginal concerns. One dance told the story of the stolen generation of children taken from their parents, forced into boarding schools, and stripped of their language and culture. Afterward, Uncle Paul, of the older generation, got up to speak. "We don't tell you these things to make you feel guilty," he said. "But now that you know about the past, we are responsible for creating a better future together."

Brokenness and pain are not the end of the story. Jesus invites us into the reality that even in the middle of difficulty, if we have the courage to name and sit with our pain, we may experience healing and solace. This Beatitude invites us to move from avoiding pain to facing what is difficult in our lives: *Blessed are those who mourn, for they will be comforted.*

May we face our pain, sit and weep, wait for comfort and healing and walk in the way of lament.

3

The Way of Humility

See Your True Self,
Bow to the Dignity of All

Blessed are the meek,
for they will inherit the earth.

MATTHEW 5:5

When my son Isaiah was three, he said, "Dad, watch me, I can run fast." He would sprint down the block making swooshing noises like a cartoon superhero. One day his older siblings said, "We can run even faster than you." They challenged him to a race. Suddenly his sense of identity was called into question.

From an early age we wonder, *Who am I?* and we begin to form our identity by making comparisons. Am I a boy or a girl? Am I short or tall? Am I slow or fast? We don't just notice these differences. We assign value and worth to ourselves based on what we discover.

Social comparison theory explains how we build our sense of self by asking, "Who is better or worse off than me?" In one experiment, participants played a game. The reward center of their brains became more activated seeing other players lose than it did by winning. In another study, participants listened to a story about an enviable person's success. When details were added about the person's failures, the listener's brain reward centers lit up. We seem to feel better about ourselves when we delight in other people's demise.

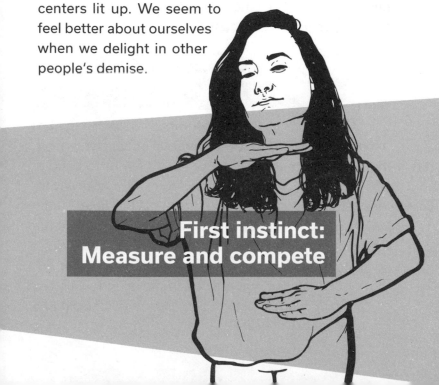

First instinct:
Measure and compete

Our first instinct is to compare and compete for a sense of identity. Who is the tallest? The strongest? The smartest? The best looking? Am I greater than or less than you? Metaphorically, we hold up our hands to measure and compare. That's the instinct of measuring and competing. Which of us is the most successful? Intelligent? Wealthy? Lovable? Ethical? Creative? When we come out on top, we feel good. When we come out on the bottom, we feel less than. Some of us work hard to be the best. Others give up trying and are resigned to being less than. The time we spend striving to defend or dismiss our worth is exhausting.

Where do you struggle with competition or comparisons? How do you get caught in the trap of feeling greater than or less than others?

I can go from feeling greater than to less than in a nanosecond. I tend to feel superior to people who don't manage their money well. But I feel inferior to people who have more wealth than I do. I think I am relatively fit for a person my age—and that makes me feel good—until I meet someone who is in much better shape. I'm grateful for the opportunities I have as a teacher and writer. But I am jealous and insecure when I hear about another author's book sales or higher speaking fees. To feel better I'll switch up what is being compared: *well, at least I'm not a sellout like they are!*

I am aware of my unearned privileges. As a straight white male I am treated with politeness and respect almost everywhere I go. With all the advantages I have, I still struggle with identity. Affirming worth can be even more challenging when your race, class, or gender identity is marginalized. It takes resilience to maintain self-respect when you speak up and your voice is ignored, when you are stopped by police without cause, when security follows you suspiciously through the store, or when people at work automatically assume you are on the cleaning crew because of your race or skin color.

In Western culture we like to believe that our achievements are primarily based on individual effort and intelligence. We celebrate the wealthy and powerful "winners" and blame the less fortunate "losers" for society's problems. Surveys suggest that the majority of us believe we are above average even though, mathematically, only half of us can be. There is a growing gap in the United States and the United Kingdom between the rich and the poor. This has a surprising effect on psychological and physical well-being. Data suggest that inequality and negative comparisons lead to higher rates of mental and physical illness, homicides, violent crime, and shorter life expectancies—even for the wealthiest people in these countries! In their book *The Spirit Level* Richard Wilkinson and Kate Pickett suggest that due to negative comparisons, a low-income person in a rich country often feels less well-off than a much poorer person in a low-income country.

We are hurt by the urge to compare and compete. As an ancient philosopher wryly observed, "All toil and all achievement spring from one person's envy of another." Comparison and competition drive global consumerism and increasing public and private debt. A prideful position of dominance is a primary cause of ecological destruction and climate change. When we feel less than, it compels us to want more, at any cost.

Is comparing ourselves to one another a secure and stable way to build a sense of identity and worth? It is developmentally necessary but ultimately unfulfilling. No matter what we achieve there will always be someone who bumps us out of the ranking. Most sports records are eventually broken. Accomplishments are surpassed or forgotten. Beauty and fame fade with time.

Can we find a better way? What if we could get out of the game of competition and comparisons? Imagine having self-respect that is not dependent on winning or being better? What would that be like? Is that something you would like to experience?

We are being invited to move from what is instinctual to a deeper consciousness that can transform us and create a better world.

In his teaching on the hill, Jesus said, "Blessed are the meek, for they will inherit the earth." Because *meekness* sounds like *weakness*, it is often misconstrued to mean passive submission. A more accurate definition is *strength under control*. When you know your inherent worth, you can be at ease, not striving or competing or feeling inferior to anyone. Another's person's ranking does not diminish your value or esteem.

What is the deepest and truest thing about you? The Hebrew Scriptures point to the reality that we are made in the divine image. You have inherent dignity and worth—value that is not dependent on your achievements or validation from others. What matters more than anything is the value you have in the eyes of the Creator. This awareness prompted the ancient poet to write:

> I praise you because I am fearfully and
> > wonderfully made;
> > your works are wonderful,
> > I know that full well.

The Posture of Honoring Inherent Worth

Most ancient and traditional cultures have postures and ritualized practices for showing respect and honoring the sacred: bowing the head, lifting the hands, or falling prostrate to the ground. You are being invited to honor the sacredness that is at the core of your being. Imagine putting your hand on your heart as a reminder that you are fearfully and wonderfully made. Then bow forward to respect the sacred source of your life and acknowledge the equal dignity of others.

There is a story about Jesus when he was the guest of honor at a feast. He got up during the dinner and washed the feet of his followers. They were incensed. It was the job of a household servant to wash the feet of guests when they arrived. It was the most humble job, not fit for a great rabbi. Jesus washing the feet of his disciples is often seen as an incredible example of humility. But the story also reveals how his disciples were stuck in rigid, false, hierarchical thinking. They resisted having him wash their feet because they divided the world into greater than and less than. Jesus knew his own dignity and worth, and he washed his friends' feet because he knew their equal dignity and worth.

We see in the life of Jesus flexibility that comes from an accurate understanding of worth. He poured out his life for others and also let others care for him. He asked for help, a drink of water, from a woman his own culture despised. He depended on friends for funds, food, and shelter as he traveled. He also let others wash his feet.

On the road to Jerusalem, where Jesus would be executed, his disciples argued about which one of them was the greatest. In response Jesus said, "The greatest among you should be like the youngest, and the one who rules like the one who serves. . . . I am among you as one who serves." He invites us into a community of interdependence where we all need help and we all have something to give.

New posture:
Honor
inherent
worth

Learning to Bow to the Dignity of All

What practices might help us move from competition and comparisons to valuing true worth?

Bow to the sacred source of your life. In Western culture we tend to put ourselves at the center of the universe and see nature from a mechanistic perspective. But if we take the time to watch the sunset or gaze upon the starry night, we begin to see our existence with a more accurate scale and perspective. We are small in comparison to the vast plains, mountains, and oceans. We did not make ourselves. An unseen force or ultimate cause brought us into existence. Pausing to contemplate this, the proper response is awe.

Denise Champion, an Adnyamathanha elder, invited Lisa and me to go "on country" with her. We left in darkness and drove the empty roads north toward Wilpena Pound. Herds of leaping kangaroos peppered the landscape. Just before sunrise Aunty Denise asked us to stop the car. We pulled over just as the sun came over the horizon. "I want to greet the morning Creator has given to us," she said. She stood facing the sun and held her hands high in the air, singing praise to *Arrawantanha* (the Most High).

Afterward, Aunty Denise turned to us and said, "Thank you for joining me today. The troubles of my people weigh heavily on me. My heart has needed to be on the land of my ancestors. We say, *Yarta Wandatha*, the land is speaking. As an Aboriginal woman, I've spent much of my life thinking I was a second-class person, worthless garbage. But at sixty-two-years-old, I'm slowly realizing that I'm not junk. I am a beloved child of God. I bear the image of the divine!"

I know the courage it took for Aunty Denise to speak these words. And when she did, I noticed her standing a little taller, holding her head high in confidence. I can't help but think that being on country and offering praise to the Most High helps her get a more accurate sense of worth.

Bow to affirm your dignity and worth. It can take time to internalize your true value and worth. Most of us have rehearsed distorted statements like, "I have to be the best or I'm nothing," or "I'm not worth much and my voice doesn't matter. Stay small." These patterns of thinking can be challenged and replaced with more accurate self-talk. If you struggle to affirm your true dignity and worth, you might consider taking on the practice of pausing several times a day to speak words of worth aloud.

PRACTICE *Affirming worth.* Try speaking these words out loud as you bow and hold your hand to your heart: *I am made in the divine image, a creature of inherent dignity and worth.*

Saying words like these can sound almost too good to be true. But how would our lives be different if we learned to live from such deep confidence? It may feel unnatural at first, but gradually you will internalize the truth of who you are.

Bow to honor the dignity and worth of others. After Jesus washed his disciples' feet he said, "You also should wash one another's feet. I have set you an example that you should do as I have done for you."

To better understand the way of humility, at Ninefold Path events I often invite people to wash each other's feet. For most of us, washing feet is less about cleaning dirt away and more about the dynamic intimacy of the interaction. The act is confronting. Some of us don't like to be touched. Others feel embarrassed by the smell or appearance of their feet. To make it slightly less awkward I often invite two people to wash a third person's feet together.

When I offered to wash Kevin's feet, he was in a drug and alcohol recovery program after living on the street for several years. Hesitantly he took off his shoes and socks. He told me he felt bad that I had to see his "ugly feet" that were swollen and covered in varicose veins. It was a bold step to allow me to see this vulnerable part of himself. I said, "Brother, I am happy to wash your feet." Tenderly I cleaned and then gently massaged them with essential oil. As I did, I looked into his eyes and said, "Kevin, I want you to know that you are valuable and precious. You are made in the divine image. You have inherent dignity and worth." Tears began streaming down his cheeks. The combination of words and touch heightened the impact of the moment we shared. Sometimes we need others to help us internalize our true dignity and worth.

After washing each other's feet I often ask, "Which did you find more challenging—having your feet washed or washing someone else's feet?" Nearly everyone says that having their feet washed was more stretching. Since most of us no longer walk dusty roads in sandals, what might be the twenty-first-century equivalent of washing one another's feet? Allowing a friend to help you clean your bathroom? Inviting someone into a private part of your life where you need help? It would need to be something that invites intimacy and vulnerability and meets a practical need.

Bow to give and receive help. There are a lot of misconceptions about meekness or humility. Some people think it means letting other people take advantage of you, always saying yes or always taking the serving role. Some of us have formed our personalities around being "the helper" and making ourselves indispensable. This can look like humility but often comes from a secret source of pride: *I* need *you* to need *me*. If we aren't careful, our desire to help can disempower the person we hope to serve.

When we live in a binary of greater than and less than, it makes it hard to connect authentically. Years ago my friend Eric directed a community center where low-income people and those experiencing homelessness could get meals and groceries. When I showed up to volunteer I expected to be put in charge of some area because of my background. Instead, Eric directed me to a Black trans woman named Sandra. He said, "Mark, Sandra is your section leader and will show you how to bag up food for our guests." At the end of the day Sandra handed me a bag of groceries to take home. At first I declined, thinking that someone else could use the groceries more than I. But Sandra said, "Honey this here is a community. We all have something to give and we all have something we need. Take the food home to your babies."

If you notice power differentials in your interactions, find some way to equalize the relationship. My friend Jeremy lives in East Africa in a patriarchal society where men, and particularly the male head of the household, are accustomed to being served by their wives and children (and domestic workers). When I invited Jeremy to join me in experimenting with the way of humility, he immediately knew what this could look like in his situation. He committed to shop for groceries and cook the evening meal for his wife, children, and their domestic employees each night for a week. And he even cleaned up the dishes! In his culture this was a radical expression of the way of humility.

Which do you find easier or more difficult: giving help or asking for help? For those of us who prefer to be in the helping role, asking for and receiving help might be the more transformative action.

When you are fully at home with yourself, you don't have to push forward to seek status or importance. This is why Jesus told his disciples, when you are invited to a party, don't look for the best table. "Take the lowest place, so that when your host comes, [they] will say to you, 'Friend, move up to a better place.' . . . Those who exalt themselves will be humbled, and those who humble themselves will be exalted."

Imagine if we all chose to use our strength to serve and not to oppress, to wash the dirt from each other's feet. In the end it won't be the proud strivers who inherit the earth but those who embrace the reality of equal dignity and cooperation. They will go ahead together. This Beatitude invites us to move from competition and comparisons to true worth: *Blessed are the meek, for they will inherit the earth.*

May we stop striving, see our true selves, bow to the dignity of all, and walk in the way of humility.

4

The Way of Justice

Ache for Change, Step into Action

*Blessed are those who hunger and thirst
for [justice], for they [will] be satisfied.*

MATTHEW 5:6 ESV

Something deep inside tells us that the world is not as it should be. Nations go to war over land rights. Children starve because of unjust governments. Refugees struggle to survive. Many are marginalized and mistreated because of their race, class, or identity. We feel the pain of injustice. We want things to be different and better. We ache for change.

What hunger for justice is inside of you? How would you like to see the world become different and better?

It is significant to give voice to what we want to see made new. But can the world be different than it is? In the face of overwhelming struggles it's easy to live under the illusion of futility. You walk by a person begging for spare change. Will a sandwich or a dollar really make a difference? What about the larger systems? This person needs access to medication and health care, affordable housing, and work or financial support. Like me, maybe you've tried to help but gotten frustrated or over-whelmed. You might have decided, *Never again*.

Learned helplessness is a term psychologists used to describe this phenomenon. When faced with difficult tasks or situations beyond our control, we easily become discouraged, quit trying, and avoid similar challenges in the future. Apathy and passive indifference manifest in depression, passivity, procrastination, and a failure to ask for or expect help.

Our first instinct is to feel powerless. We tend to throw up our hands in resignation and think, *What can one person possibly do?* While all of us struggle with apathy, certain personalities are particularly vulnerable to feeling powerless. In a world that seems overwhelming, they make themselves small to keep the peace. Why clean the house when it will only get dirty again? Why express what you want or need when your voice will be ignored?

Religious people, and Christians in particular, have a mixed record when it comes to participating in social change. Historically, people of faith were at the forefront of antislavery and civil rights efforts. But at the same time many White Christians used Scripture to justify slavery and racial hierarchy. A false dichotomy between the spiritual and temporal is often used to rationalize the instinct of passive indifference. In the face of injustice I often hear people say things like:

- ▶ It's a sign of the times; things are supposed to go from bad to worse.

- ▶ What do you expect? We're sinners, incapable of doing anything good.

- ▶ Our country won't change until hearts are changed, so rather than working for change through laws or policies, I'm praying that God will change hearts.

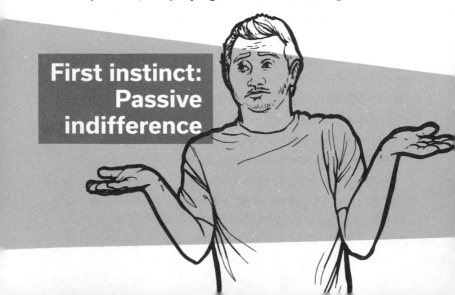

First instinct: Passive indifference

Perhaps we minimize our agency to downplay responsibility. As a collective we have often used power destructively. We've been selfish, greedy, fearful, violent, and punishing.

Imagine how the world could be if we learned to use our power for good? What if instead of numbing out to the suffering of the world, we work together to make things right? What might that be like? Is that something you would like to be a part of?

In the teaching on the hill Jesus said, "Blessed are those who hunger and thirst for [justice], for they [will] be satisfied." Human beings are powerful creatures. We are not helpless or hopeless. This is why Jesus said, "You are the light of the world. . . . Let your light shine before others, that they may see your good deeds and [praise your Creator]." These words dare us to believe in our own agency and participate in making the world what it could be—what we long for it to be.

At the beginning of his public life Jesus stood up in the synagogue and used Scripture to declare his purpose as a liberator: "The Spirit of the Lord is on me . . . to proclaim good news to the poor, . . . freedom for the prisoners . . . to set the oppressed free." He brought healing and hope to people suffering physically and mentally. He spoke truth to power, turning over tables and chasing out the currency vendors taking advantage of the poor. He taught his followers a new ethic of love, believing human suffering could be alleviated if people chose his life-giving way.

The Posture of Embracing the Power to Do Good

Imagine crossing your arms and holding them up as a symbol of your power to do good. Think Wonder Woman or Wakanda (not a stance of violence but of strength and confidence). That's the posture of embracing the power to do good. More than any generation before us, we are aware that everything is connected. We shape the world through our choices. What we do matters. So change begins with us. Each day brings us new opportunities to take action, to use our power for good. To live by doing to others what we would have them do for us. To love our neighbors as we love ourselves.

Learning to Ache for Change and Step into Action

What practices might help us move from apathy to agency?

Step into action by owning your identity as a liberator.
Whether we know it or not, we hunger for God's kingdom to be realized—the good dreams of the Creator for all of creation. Jesus spoke about the kingdom of God as a present reality. He told people, "The kingdom of heaven has come near." When asked when the kingdom of God would come, he said, "The Kingdom of God is within you." He invited his disciples to make healing the world their highest priority: "Seek first the kingdom of God and [God's justice]."

How does the world become better? When we decide to use our power for good. The whole universe is God's creative realm. We have been given a small piece of that as our personal "kingdom" to manage. Our bodies. Our minds. Our time. Our money and possessions and the influence we have in relationships. We are being invited to adopt a new identity as agents of liberation. We are invited to care about everything our Creator cares about: the dignity of human life at every stage, care of creation for future generations, just and sustainable economic policies, and care of immigrants and the poor, to name a few.

New posture: Embrace the power to do good

Step into action by imagining the world as it could be.
"Do to others what you would have them do to you" is
one way Jesus described how to exercise our power for
good. Here's a thought exercise I use to help me imagine
the good that I can do. On a sheet of paper I write, *I want
to live in a world where*, and then I write, *So one thing I
can do is*. Here are a few examples:

- ▶ *I want to live in a world where* everyone has the
  basic resources they need to thrive.

  So one thing I can do is adopt consumption limits
  and a standard of living that can be shared by most
  people on the planet, rather than just a few.

- ▶ *I want to live in a world where* future generations
  have an inhabitable planet to live on.

  So one thing I can do is limit my fossil fuel usage,
  reduce waste, and adopt a primarily plant-based diet.

- ▶ *I want to live in a world where* women are treated
  with dignity and their voices are respected.

  So one thing I can do is listen with humility and amplify the important contributions of women I know.

- ▶ *I want to live in a world where* people of every
  race and class are welcomed, included, and given
  opportunity.

  So one thing I can do is prioritize friendships and
  work partnerships with people whose race and class

backgrounds are different from my own, and learn from the wisdom and experience of minority voices.

▸ *I want to live in a world where* workers are paid a just wage for their labor.

So one thing I can do is buy products that are fair trade and slavery-free, and advocate for equitable wages in my workplace.

In some cases it's relatively easy to find a tangible action to take. With other cases you may have to wrestle a bit and brainstorm with others who share your dreams and concerns. What are the issues of justice you feel most passionate about? What practical steps can you take to help create the world you want to live in?

Step into action by making small changes. History books highlight the heroic actions of a courageous few. But equally important are small actions taken by many that lead to structural changes. The slave trade in the United Kingdom was largely abolished because many people decided to take their tea without sugar (a slave-related commodity). Women in the United States and the United Kingdom gained the right to vote because of the persistence of thousands of suffragists. The number of people living in extreme poverty has decreased by half in the past thirty years partly due to individual sponsors supporting holistic child development. Today more people have access to clean water than ever before. Though we still have a long way to go, we can celebrate the progress that has been made.

Just mentioning the potential to take new action can bring up defensiveness or shame. What if I don't want to drive less or adopt a plant-based diet? We've all been around that annoying new convert who lectures everyone else about their choices. Shame and shoulds are not healthy or effective motivators. The opportunity to make the world what it could be is a joyful invitation, not a drudging obligation. Try something new, and gradually your new actions will become healthy habits.

PRACTICE *One small step.* What is one small change you've been invited to make but haven't yet put into action? What is keeping you from doing that today? Go meatless. Walk instead of driving. Carry water from home instead of buying plastic bottles. Only consume fair-trade coffee, tea, and chocolate. Changes are easier to make when you tell someone else and do it with them—so invite a friend to join you.

Step into action by joining the struggle for justice. Small personal changes are a start, but we also need to address larger struggles for human flourishing. This requires disruption and dismantling of unjust systems and structures. And this requires collective action. We can be inspired by the words of the prophet Isaiah:

Learn to do right; seek justice.
Defend the oppressed.
Take up the cause of the fatherless;
plead the case of the widow.

Where is the struggle for justice happening now where you live?

In August 2014 the case of Michael Brown, a Missouri teenager shot and killed by police, polarized the United States. In the afternoon the not-guilty verdict was pronounced, my social media page blew up with comments supporting and criticizing the Black Lives Matter movement. That night at dinner our family talked about the ruling, and I made an offhand comment, "I'm not going to post anything about this on social media—that's just slacktivism." My daughter Hailey quickly spoke up, "But Papa, if you have a voice you should use it to amplify the voices of the oppressed."

Since I'm usually the one making dinnertime speeches, her words took me aback. We could hear the news helicopters circling overhead ready to cover the demonstration forming at the subway station a few blocks away. I said, "Okay, I hear you—but if I'm going to say something, I want to speak from firsthand experience. Let's listen and join in the cries of our neighbors."

We left the table and walked to the station. Hundreds of our neighbors were gathered to lament the ruling, and we joined their chants and prayers. A young Black man spoke like an ancient prophet. Tears welled up in my eyes. This was faith in action, where it really matters—the divine name invoked on the streets, amidst pain.

In December I went to a gathering where leaders of color spoke about ways their families have been impacted by racism. A friend told me about a time he was speaking at a university and was mistaken for the janitor and asked to clean up a mess in the bathroom. Another friend told me she had just had the "driving while Black" talk with her teenage son to help him stay alive when he is inevitably stopped by the police. My heart broke.

Two months later, while sitting in the living room with my kids, I heard gunshots. Around the corner our neighbor had been shot and killed by two undercover officers. Amilcar Perez-Lopez was a twenty-year-old undocumented immigrant who worked two jobs to support his family living in the mountains of Guatemala.

Police have a difficult job to do, but these particular officers made a series of mistakes that cost my neighbor his life—and then they lied about it. They did not clearly identify themselves and then physically overpowered Amilcar. In self-defense he pulled out a kitchen knife. When they drew their guns, he dropped the knife and turned to run. Startled, the officers fired six bullets into Amilcar's back. They immediately blocked off the street, told onlookers, "You didn't see anything here," and went door to door, seizing cameras and cell phones. They had the body removed from the crime scene before the district attorney could conduct an investigation.

Within days I consulted a lawyer. I filed a statement with the Office of Citizen Complaints and participated in a faith-leader press conference on the steps of city hall. I went to Amilcar's funeral, and we sent money to his family. We began hosting bilingual planning meetings with neighbors and helped organize vigils and marches covered by the media. A group of us held weekly prayer vigils for a year in front of the police station, pleading for the DA to indict the officers who killed Amilcar.

I spent many hours in meetings with the district attorney, speaking at police commission meetings, and attending federal justice department panels. I often wondered if our efforts were making any difference. Amilcar's death was one in a series of police killings in San Francisco while the police department was under investigation for a racist text scandal. Eventually, the chief of police was forced to resign. Amilcar's family received a settlement from the city. In 2019 the state of California passed legislation to reform use-of-force law, making it more difficult for police to shoot civilians with impunity. This was a step forward, though much more is needed. I believe that if that law had been in place earlier my neighbor might still be alive, or at least the officers who killed him would have been held more accountable.

I regret that it took me so long to act in solidarity for racial justice and police reform. I have a voice inside of me that says, *If I haven't experienced it, it can't be real,* and *If I didn't start it or can't be in charge, then it's not worth my time.* I am not the public face of the efforts I've been part of. There are many other people whose faces should be seen and voices heard before mine. It's my job to work behind the scenes, doing what I can and making the struggle known to more people who look like me.

It's easy to feel less urgency about changing unjust systems when they benefit us or we are insulated from the pain they cause. James, the brother of Jesus wrote, "If anyone, then, knows the good they ought to do and doesn't do it, it is sin for them." If we aren't actively working for change on both personal and systemic levels, then we are complicit in keeping things the way they are. The system is indeed broken, but we are that system. If we want to see change, it will have to begin with us—with our hearts and minds, our actions, our voices, and our votes. This Beatitude invites us to move from apathy to agency: *Blessed are those who hunger and thirst for [justice], for they [will] be satisfied.*

May we ache for change, embrace our power to do good, step into action, and walk in the way of justice.

5

The Way of Compassion

Stop Judging, Look with Love

Blessed are the merciful,
for they will be shown mercy.

MATTHEW 5:7

As a child, when you watched a movie or TV show, did you wonder, *Who's the good guy and who's the bad guy?* We want to see the good guy win and the bad guy lose and get what they deserve. You probably asked a similar question about yourself: *Am I a good boy or a bad boy?* or *Am I a good girl or a bad girl?* This is how we develop a moral compass. We expect there to be a direct relationship between actions and consequences. If I'm good, I'll be rewarded. If I'm bad, I'll be punished.

Most of us live with a sense that something inside us is broken. We don't always treat other people the way we want to be treated, and people don't always treat us with the love and respect we feel we deserve. Our sense of fairness or right and wrong is violated.

When someone does wrong or breaks the rules, our first instinct is to judge them and feel contempt toward them. This impulse is embodied in various ancient codes of reciprocity: "Eye for eye and tooth for tooth." Tit for tat. Whatever you do to me, I will exact similar vengeance on you. This primitive though necessary level of moral reasoning continues to shape our interactions, legal system, and foreign policy. We "cancel" public figures when they are accused of wrongdoing. We send people to prison to be punished for their crimes. Airstrikes are ordered to retaliate for what our enemies have done (or plan to do). This mentality expresses a retributive rather than restorative understanding of justice.

Those of us with perfectionistic personality tendencies are particularly troubled by not living up to our own standards, no matter how hard we try. And we are angry that others can't seem to follow the rules as we do. The physical embodiment of this judgment is the downward glance and pointing finger. A character from an old Canadian sketch comedy perfectly embodies this instinct. Standing in a public square "the Headcrusher" holds up two fingers, looks with contempt at a person, and declares "I crush you, I'm crushing your head," while pinching his fingers together. We often feel obliged to judge or despise others or ourselves.

How we handle our mistakes matters. We can allow our failures to define us and live with self-loathing, shame, and resentment. Or we can let go of the desire to punish or take revenge. Learning to make judgments may be developmentally necessary but is ultimately a toxic way to live. What if we could learn to let go of our resentments, contempt, and the need to be right? What if you could finally forgive yourself? What would that be like? Is that a quality of life you would like to experience?

In the teaching on the hill Jesus said, "Blessed are the merciful, for they will be shown mercy." This Beatitude promises that as we learn to see others through eyes of compassion we will experience the love and unconditional

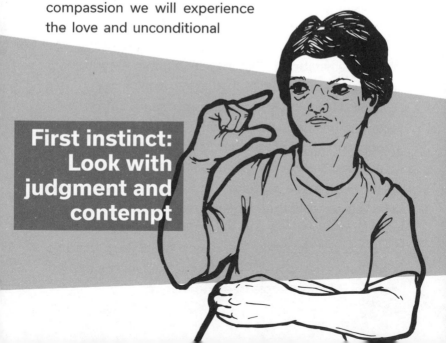

First instinct: Look with judgment and contempt

acceptance we so desperately long for. The reality is that we are deeply loved. Mercy triumphs over judgment, promising us kindness that goes beyond the consequences of our actions or the retribution we feel others deserve. Mercy dares us to believe that the truest thing about us is not that we are broken or flawed but that we are beloved.

 What in your life do you need mercy for? Who needs your forgiveness?

The Posture of Seeing with Compassion

Imagine making the shape of a valentine heart with your hands and holding it up to your face. That's the posture of seeing with compassion. You might picture yourself looking through the heart at a person you struggle to forgive, remembering that they are beloved. Or you could imagine yourself being looked at in a similar way.

When I teach on the way of compassion, I often invite people to pair up, make the shape of a heart with their hands, and stare into each other's eyes. We don't often look at each other so intently. People chuckle uncomfortably. After the giggling subsides, I say, "Remember who you are looking at. A being made in the divine image who is deeply loved. See them for who they really are. Precious and beloved. How does it feel to look with this intention? How does it feel to be seen with such tenderness?" Many people begin to tear up.

Once I invited a group to do this and noticed that a young woman sitting near me was blind. Suddenly I realized these postures don't work for everyone. I wanted her to feel included, so I went over and whispered, "Would you be comfortable having me touch your face?" She consented. "You can also touch mine if you like," I added. We sat there for a few precious moments holding each other's faces, acknowledging one another's belovedness. It was an experience I will never forget. We need each other's help to embrace the tangible reality of grace.

We are being invited to see each other from a new level of consciousness. Jesus explained this by saying, "Do not judge. . . . For in the same way you judge others, you will be judged, and with the measure you use, it will

New posture:
See with
compassion

be measured to you." People once pressured Jesus to pronounce judgment on a woman who had been caught in adultery. Instead of joining their contempt he said, "Let any one of you who is without [guilt] be the first to throw a stone at her." Instead of focusing on other people's behavior, we are invited to own our mistakes and failures, knowing that we need grace ourselves. Someone who understands their need for mercy naturally extends mercy to others.

Many of us struggle to believe that God looks at us with mercy instead of pointing the finger. An ancient psalm reads,

> The LORD is compassionate and gracious,
>   slow to anger, abounding in love. . . .
> As a [parent] has compassion on [their] children,
>   so the LORD has compassion.

When my daughter, Hailey, was young she drew pictures for me, which I received with a parent's delight: "Wow, you used lots of green crayon in this one! Thank you!" But gradually she became more self-conscious about the quality of her pictures. She reasoned, *My dad is good at drawing, so my drawings also have to be good.* One day I found her at her desk crying next to a wastebasket full of crumpled paper. In her mind none of her pictures were good enough. What Hailey didn't understand then was that my pleasure wasn't dependent on her drawings being perfect. Since the moment she was born I've felt a depth of love for her that I hardly knew existed. Nothing could dampen the enthusiasm I have for my beloved child. Sometimes she still catches me gazing at her. "Dad, what are you looking at?" she asks. And I say, "I'm looking at my child, in whom is all my delight!" Because of my experience as a parent, I find it easy to believe that the Creator delights in each of us.

Learning to Look with Love

What practices might help us move from judgment and contempt to the way of compassion?

Look with love by seeing with eyes of compassion. A politician's name comes up in conversation and you feel contempt. Someone walks into the room and negative thoughts and feelings arise. You pass someone on the street and immediately start to evaluate, label, or judge: fat, skinny, ugly, attractive, smart, dumb, rich, poor, safe, dangerous. With practice most of us have become very good at looking with contempt.

Those who wrote about Jesus took note of the particular way he looked at people: "When he saw the crowds, he had compassion on them." "Jesus looked at him and loved him." "When the Lord saw her, his heart went out to her." Jesus combined the physical act of seeing with the heart discipline of love. Like a muscle that can be strengthened, we can train to see with eyes of compassion. I try practicing this when I am walking down the street or am in a crowd. I look into the face of each person and silently whisper, *Child of God, may you be well.* This interrupts my normal tendency to label and judge. I take a second look and choose to see people for who they truly are—*Beloved*. This practice radically changes my interactions. I am more open and less self-conscious.

Look with love by practicing positive speech. How we talk also reveals a lot about how we see ourselves and others. In Ninefold Path groups I invite people to join me in a commitment to practice positive speech. We make this agreement together: *I promise to practice positive speech. For the next seven days I will only speak words of compassion and affirmation about myself and others. I will avoid making critical or disparaging comments.*

When I made this commitment recently, I broke my promise three times in the first three hours. I gossiped. I talked disparagingly about someone. And I spoke with disdain about a politician. I didn't beat myself up about this failure. The goal is to become more self-aware so I can make new choices. I'm still learning to fully internalize the reality of grace.

PRACTICE *Positive speech.* Would you consider making a promise to practice positive speech right now? Who can you share this commitment with?

Look with love by letting go of resentments. When my friend Patrick was eleven, South Sudanese soldiers entered his village and forced the men to join their army. His older brother refused, and Patrick watched as soldiers hacked his brother's body to pieces with a machete. Patrick has had to work to let go of his resentment toward the men who killed his brother. At some point most of us have to work through a process of letting go of resentments toward people who have hurt us or those we love. A promise was broken, harsh words were spoken, or you were treated in a way that violated your dignity.

In my first full-time job I worked at an inner-city mission that served at-risk children, families, and people without housing. It was challenging and rewarding. But on several occasions I saw the director, my boss, hit or scream at people in our programs. When I confronted her about this, she said, "You are so young and sensitive. You can't let every little thing upset you." When I told a mentor what I'd witnessed, they discouraged me from reporting the incidents to child protective services— reasoning that doing so would shut down the center and the vital services it provided (advice I now regret taking). The next time I saw the director mistreat someone, I gently confronted her. She punched me in the stomach, beat me to the ground, and humiliated me in front of the other staff. I left the lunchroom in tears. When I quit a few weeks later she spread horrible rumors about me.

I spent the next few months unemployed and reeling from this trauma. I couldn't sleep, and my anger spilled over into other relationships. For the next two years I rehearsed my resentments to anyone who would listen. "Can you believe what she did to me—and to those children! What injustice!" I find it hardest to forgive people who I trusted would treat me with kindness and respect. I also am aware that I have disappointed and hurt people who trusted me: family members, close friends, and people who have had me as their boss.

What are signs that you are struggling to forgive someone?

▸ You can't stop thinking about them and get worked up whenever they come to mind.

▸ You end up sharing your grievance about them with anyone who will listen and try to control others' opinions of that person.

▸ You secretly relish the possibility that something bad will happen to them.

▸ You assume the worst about the person and ignore signs of their nobility.

▸ You go out of your way to avoid them or find it difficult to look into their eyes.

What does it mean to forgive? Forgiveness is an intentional process of giving up my anger and resentment toward someone who has hurt me—so that I no longer wish for or seek revenge. I am increasingly able to wish them well.

There are a lot of misconceptions about forgiveness. Forgiving someone doesn't mean condoning, excusing, or forgetting the offending behavior. The pain may stay with you for a long time. Forgiving someone doesn't mean trust is restored. You can forgive someone and still ask that they face the consequences of their actions. Forgiveness isn't contingent on the other person apologizing. You can forgive someone even if they won't apologize or are unable to acknowledge the hurt they have caused. But forgiveness is not the same as reconciliation. Reconciliation requires both parties to work together to repair the relationship by admitting wrongdoing, offering forgiveness, and making amends to restore trust. Forgiveness is also a process, not a one-time event. Every time I remember the hurt, I have an opportunity to let go again. The following are some steps that have helped me work through this process.

1. Name and explore the hurt. It can be easier to forgive when you feel permission to grieve the pain you have experienced. Instead of indiscriminately venting your resentment to anyone who will listen, it can help to choose one trusted person to process your pain with. That person can listen empathetically, validate your experience, and help you clarify your feelings. It can also help to journal. Here are some good questions to explore:

- ▶ How would I describe the wrong done to me?
- ▶ What feelings did their actions trigger?
- ▶ How did their actions touch a vulnerable place inside of me?

2. Examine your attachment to the resentment. Perhaps you've heard the adage "Resentment is like drinking poison and expecting someone else to get sick and die." It takes a lot of energy to be resentful, and it can make you sick. Research suggests that people who harbor long-term anger and resentment are at an increased risk for high blood pressure, elevated heart rate, chronic inflammation, and compromised immunity. They are more likely to die of heart disease. The invitation to forgive can seem costly, but it's even more costly to hold on to bitterness. There is real freedom in letting go. *How is holding on to resentment shaping your life? What do you hope to gain? Why are you struggling to forgive? How might you benefit from letting go?*

3. Develop greater understanding of the person who wronged you. Our wounds, fears, and limitations shape the way we treat each other. We usually don't intend to hurt people, but sometimes our thoughts and actions are misguided. While Jesus was being executed, he cried out, "Father, forgive them, for they do not know what they are doing." It helps me to think about the circumstances and pressures that shaped the person who wronged me. My boss at the mission had spent fifty years working with people in addiction and crisis. She was likely a victim of trauma herself and hadn't found healing.

4. See the pain from a larger perspective. If the person who hurt you continues in their behavior, ultimately things will not go well for them. They will experience the logical consequences of their actions. "A [person] reaps what [they] sow." You don't have to retaliate or take revenge yourself. Justice will be served on a cosmic level. God treats us better than our actions deserve. To complete the circle we must want the same for the person who hurt us. This is why Jesus taught his disciples to pray, "Forgive us our sins, for we also forgive everyone who sins against us."

5. Look with love by practicing self-compassion. Sometimes the hardest person to forgive is yourself. You might think that being hard on yourself will motivate you to do better. This rarely helps. Punishing yourself for mistakes and failures usually perpetuates a cycle of negative behavior. To live better we are invited to practice self-compassion. *What would you tell a friend who is struggling to forgive themselves?* Listen to your answer and be gentle with yourself. Kindness leads us to change.

Being merciful takes strength and courage and opens us to the possibility that we (and others) can grow and change. This Beatitude invites to move from judgment and contempt to mercy and compassion: *Blessed are the merciful, for they will be shown mercy.*

May we stop judging, remember we are beloved, look with love, and walk in the way of compassion.

6

The Way of Right Motive

Choose Goodness, Show the Real You

> *Blessed are the pure in heart,*
> *for they will see God.*
> MATTHEW 5:8

I was having breakfast with a family when their young daughter handed me a drawing of a dinosaur along with a note: "Dear Mr. Mark, I would like you to send me a gift in the mail. Here's my address. . . ." Her parents, chagrined by her directness, began to scold her. I interrupted, "I'm glad you had the courage to tell me what you want! I'll try to honor your request." One thing I appreciate about young children is that they will tell you exactly what they are thinking and feeling. They have no filter. If they are happy, you know it. If they are sad, they cry. When they want something, they ask.

Over time we learn not to show our real thoughts and feelings. A divide comes between what is in our hearts and what we are willing to show to others. Our first instinct is to hide behind what psychologists call a "mask" or "persona." You can embody this impulse by covering your face with your hands. We wear masks for a reason. Not everything inside of us is what we would want it to be. *What would you think if you really knew who I am inside?*

Shame, the feeling of being seen and exposed, is a universal human phenomenon. The Hebrew story of Adam and Eve illustrates this archetypal loss of innocence. They ate the fruit of the tree of knowledge of good and evil. When they realized they were

**First instinct:
Hide and pretend**

seen, their impulse was to run and hide, as if they could escape the light of divine presence. In this story the humans pull away while the Creator continues to pursue relationship. "Where are you?" the Lord asks, expecting to walk with Adam and Eve in the cool of the day. They made God their enemy and judge and began living under the illusion that they could cover up what was happening in their heart.

Our world is dominated by false images and appearances. Social media has accelerated our ability to curate how we present ourselves. We share only what we think will be celebrated. Our ability to manipulate impressions creates suspicion. Can we trust what a politician or religious leader says? Are they telling the truth or creating spin to hide their true motives? Some of us, based on personality, find it particularly difficult to be seen or tell the truth about ourselves. We've become experts at performing and achieving, convinced that what we look like to others is who we really are.

I want people to think I'm intelligent, virtuous, wise, and creative. Someone gave me a pair of colorful designer sunglasses I thought conveyed this image. So I wore them all the time and used a photo of myself wearing them for promotion. Soon people expected to see me in colorful oversized glasses. Eventually, those frames wore out. I kept replacing them. Only a few people knew the truth and gently mocked me for it. One day my daughter came home with prescription reading glasses. I tried them on. Suddenly I could read the texts on my phone without squinting! After all those years faking it, I now needed glasses. This is a rather silly example of the ways we attempt to manage how we are seen by others.

> **?** How about you? What masks do you tend to wear? What is important to you about how you are seen by others?

We can become so divorced from our true selves that it's difficult to make real contact with God, ourselves, or one another. If I'm wearing my mask and you're wearing your mask, we are only relating to each other's personas. Hiding or denying our mixed motives doesn't make them go away. Shame does not help us change nor cynicism help us heal.

What if we could take off our masks and allow ourselves to be seen and known for who we really are? What would that be like? What would make that safe? Is wholehearted authenticity something you desire?

The Posture of Wholehearted Honesty

In the teaching on the hill Jesus said, "Blessed are the pure in heart, for they will see God." Purity of heart is being honest about what's inside. You give up trying to be perfect and show the real you. When we are honest with ourselves, with others, and with God, we step out of the shadows and into the light. And light transforms everything it touches. It reveals, heals, and purifies. Imagine holding your hands up to your face and spreading them apart, allowing yourself to be seen doing jazz hands! That's the posture of wholehearted honesty.

Jesus modeled wholeheartedness. He didn't try to impress people or play to the crowd. He had nothing to protect or hide. When people asked where he lived, he said, "Come and see." He invited his disciples to be with him at his most vulnerable moments. He understood the reality that God sees all and that the truth eventually

New posture: Wholehearted honesty

reveals itself: "There is nothing hidden that will not be disclosed, and nothing concealed that will not be known or brought out into the open."

Whatever is inside us eventually comes out, no matter how hard we may try to cover it up. Neurons that fire together wire together. Other pathways die off and our mind becomes less flexible. As we age we become less capable of hiding our true attitudes and thoughts. If we have cultivated worry, fear, bitterness, and judgment, it eventually leaks out—and we can be difficult to be around. But if we have practiced gratitude, joy, and selfless love, we manifest these to others. Over time we reveal what we have rehearsed in our hearts throughout our lives. The wise teacher of Proverbs said, "Above all else, guard your heart, for everything you do flows from it."

The way of right motive invites us to be honest but also to choose goodness. Honesty by itself isn't enough. I might tell you what I truly think and end up hurting you. Getting things off my chest might feel good but can be extremely damaging if my heart is full of anger, lust, jealousy, or rage. We need heart renovation or refinement. This is why the poet King David wrote, "Create in me a clean heart, O God, and renew a right spirit within me."

Learning to Choose Goodness and Tell the Truth

What practices might help us move from hiding to wholehearted authenticity?

Show the real you by telling the truth about yourself.
Telling the truth about yourself can empower you to begin to live in a new way. James, the brother of Jesus, wrote, "Confess your [mistakes and failures] to each other . . . so that you may be healed." We aren't meant to carry our burdens or struggles alone. Keeping a secret is what gives darkness its power. Sharing what's inside with at least one other person can help you become more wholehearted. A woman I met at a Ninefold Path event in Uganda felt inspired to be more honest with her spouse. She told me, "I haven't been sharing myself fully, and we've become distant. I'm feeling invited to talk more openly about my worries, doubts, needs, and desires. I believe it will help us have a more intimate and loving relationship."

You will want to pick someone you trust to be completely honest with, but this may still require taking a risk. I meet once a week with a group of friends. We are committed to telling the unvarnished truth about ourselves. These friends know me at my best and worst. We've walked with each other through experiences of failure, faith crisis, depression, and family challenges. And we celebrate our milestones and successes together.

Show the real you by being wholehearted in your decisions. We pursue right motive when we seek agreement between what we say and what we need and want. Jesus said, "Let your 'Yes' be 'Yes,' and your 'No,' 'No.'" When we say yes but mean no, it creates a divide. We often do this when we fear disappointing someone or in order to live up to an image we have of ourselves. Feeling resentful later about saying yes is often a sign of acting from a divided heart. If it's the truth, it's okay to say, "Sorry, I don't want to," "I am not able to," or "Now is not a good time." Others of us say no when we want to say yes. We often do this when we are afraid of taking a risk or losing control, but we later feel alone and regret missed opportunities. We practice healthy boundaries by learning to tell the truth about our wants and needs. *How do you experience disagreement between what you say and what your heart wants?*

Show the real you by practicing secrecy. We are being invited to pay attention to what we do and also why we do what we do. Sometimes we want to appear good more than we want to be good. Our motives are mixed. I know I am guilty of this. I go out of my way to manage people's impressions of me, posting or sharing what I believe signals my virtue. A strategy Jesus taught for becoming wholehearted is to do good in secret: "When you give to the needy, do not let your left hand know what your right hand is doing." "When you pray, . . . [don't do it] standing on the street corners to be seen by others." "When you fast . . . wash your face, so that it will not be obvious to others." Purity of heart is about doing the right thing for the right reason. Doing good without telling anyone is one way to check your motives.

One of my mentors was the professor and philosopher Dallas Willard. I learned a lot from him but was critical that he wasn't more outspoken about social justice issues. My friend Gary Black did his doctoral dissertation on Willard's work and influence. He interviewed many people, including Trevor Hudson, an author and pastor from South Africa. Trevor told Gary that during the apartheid era, Dallas encouraged key faith leaders to advocate for the release of Nelson Mandela from prison so that apartheid could be dismantled. Gary was surprised to hear this. Trevor explained, "I invited Dallas to come to teach in South Africa. I had no honorarium and asked if he would mind sleeping in a small room that we used as a sewing room. He accepted my invitation and visited three more times. Each time he taught, the numbers who came to hear him multiplied. His teaching would often affirm the need for public ethics and social responsibility, along with the need for personal transformation." When Gary interviewed Dallas's wife, Jane, about his time in South Africa, she knew little about his activities there. When Gary asked Dallas about his time in South Africa, he refused to even speak about it. That's real secrecy! I would have wanted everyone to know about my involvement in such a significant era of struggle for racial justice and human rights.

Show the real you by allowing God to see what's inside of you. You can pursue right motive by inviting God to see what's inside of you. Since ancient times seekers have cultivated intentional practices of examen, inviting the inner witness to search the mind and heart:

> Search me, God, and know my heart;
>> test me and know my anxious thoughts.
> See if there is any offensive way in me,
>> and lead me in the way everlasting.

What can we affirm about the nature of the divine being that makes it safe to step out into the light and be seen? The Hebrew-Christian Scriptures speak of the divine being as having both male and female qualities: a Creator who is intimately acquainted with human experience. Contemplative prayer can help us invite the Creator's tender gaze. Consider the possibility that the Creator of the universe is closer to you now than your very breath, living at the very center of yourself. In God "we live and move and have our being." You are not separate but intimately connected to the source of all life

PRACTICE *Examine.* Consent to the Creator seeing your thoughts and feelings, trusting this loving and compassionate gaze. What does your heart most deeply long for? What needs and longings are in your heart right now?

I was first introduced to the practice of letting God search my heart in my twenties, but it took many years for me to adopt it as a regular habit of contemplation. For a time I met with a group once a week to do fifty minutes of centering or stillness prayer. We also committed to doing twenty minutes of centering prayer each day on our own. At each meeting one of us would read a short portion of the Gospels, light a candle, and turn off the lights. Our intention was to breathe deep, be aware of the divine presence, and stay in the moment rather than letting our thoughts wander to the past or future. If I got distracted, I would use the word *Abba* or the sentence "Search me, God, and know my heart" to help me return to the present.

During one session I kept getting distracted by unwanted thoughts and shame about past mistakes. I don't often hear God's voice audibly, but at that moment I felt a whisper of invitation saying, "Let's revisit this memory you feel shame about, together."

Here's the memory. When I was young, I was intensely curious about what people looked like without their clothes on and what it would be like to have sex. One night I stopped by a gas station I knew sold adult magazines. (This was in the days before the internet.) I told the person behind the counter I wanted to buy a magazine. "Which one?" he asked jokingly. "You don't care which one I give you, do you?" He handed me the magazine in a brown paper bag. When I got to the car, I hid it under the seat. As I drove home I wondered, "What if I get into a car accident?" I kept imagining my parents coming to the crash site to identify my mangled body and discovering the magazine!

When I got home, I went to my room. It was full of reminders of my girlfriend, Lisa (who I've now been married to for thirty years). She had spent hundreds of hours stitching the quilt that lay on my bed. Her picture hung on the wall next to a framed cross-stitch she had made inscribed with *Be still and know that I am God.* I folded up the quilt, took the picture and cross-stitch down, and put them in the closet. I wanted to hide what I was doing, even from myself. After my time with the magazine, I burned it. I thought of that night as the worst thing I'd done up to that point in my life.

Under the flicker of the candlelight I invited God into this memory and wondered, *Creator, what are your thoughts and feelings about that night?* I heard a voice in my mind say, "Mark, I saw everything, and for me it is a precious memory. I gave you this overwhelming gift of your sexuality. What I see is a young person navigating that gift in the best way they knew how at the time. Did you think you could become sexually mature without making any mistakes? You look back on this as one of your worst moments, but I see it as one of your best, full of desire and curiosity. You wanted to do good."

† † †

What's inside of you is seen and held with tenderness. We are invited to step further into the light, to be authentic, wholehearted, and divided no more. This Beatitude invites us to move from hiding to wholehearted goodness: *Blessed are the pure in heart, for they will see God.*

May we drop our masks, step into the light, choose goodness, and walk in the way of right motive.

7

The Way of Peacemaking

Make Peace, Reach Past Differences

> *Blessed are the peacemakers, for they*
> *will be called children of God.*
>
> MATTHEW 5:9

Shalom and *salaam*—peace—are the most common greetings in Jewish and Muslim cultures. In Hebrew the word *shalom* suggests not only the absence of war but the possibility of wholeness, harmony, and prosperity—life as it should be and the world as it was created to be. Holiday carols echo our plea and hope for "Peace on earth" while troops advance, drones strike, and corporations build the technologies of war. Politicians argue. Families squabble. Why is it so hard for us to live in peace with one another?

We are fragile creatures. Our desire for safety and identity causes us to gravitate toward those who are most like us. We look for security and belonging by identifying with particular groups. My family. My country. My ethnicity. My religion and culture. My sports team. This dualistic thinking creates so much oppositional energy. Some personalities are particularly exacting in the lines they draw between themselves and others. Their immediate impulse is to pull away.

Our first instinct is to divide the world according to people who are like us, like what we like, and believe what we believe, and those who don't. It's an instinct of dividing by us versus them, with one hand pointing to the chest and the other held up like a stop sign. Our tendency toward opposition is rooted in our biology. Our brains are wired to more readily trust

First instinct:
Divide by us
versus them

someone who looks like us and to be suspicious of those with different facial features and skin tones. To find peace our spiritual development must transcend our biology. We need a new level of consciousness to move past dividing by us versus them.

I know how susceptible I am to a mentality of us versus them. I have a prejudice toward people with political and theological views different from my own. I'm proudly urban. We call it the City or San Francisco, never San Fran. I'm a pedestrian and cyclist. Drivers make me nervous. Some of the distinctions I make are petty and verge on the absurd. My preference is direct-trade, single-origin coffee that is dry harvested, lightly roasted, ground in a conical burr grinder, and filtered through an Aero Press with water that is exactly 195 degrees Fahrenheit. How could you like coffee prepared any other way?

 How about you? Who do you tend to place on the other side of the us-versus-them spectrum?

What if we could find a way to live beyond the divides? Imagine a world where instead of taking sides we seek common ground? What might greater peace look like in your closest relationships? Is this something you desire?

The Posture of Reaching Past Differences

In his teaching on the hill, Jesus said, "Blessed are the peacemakers, for they will be called children of God." The reality is that we are all sons and daughters of one divine parent, members of one human family. We belong to one another. There are no sides. Those who understand this naturally become peacemakers. Imagine stretching out your arms in an embrace and linking your fingers together as a symbolic posture of reaching past differences. Together we can search for common ground and work toward the common good.

Jesus reached out to connect with people typically disparaged and treated as outsiders. He aroused controversy by associating with tax collectors and others labeled as "sinners." He welcomed children, who were thought to be of less importance than adults. He touched "unclean" people, those with diseases who were believed to be contagious.

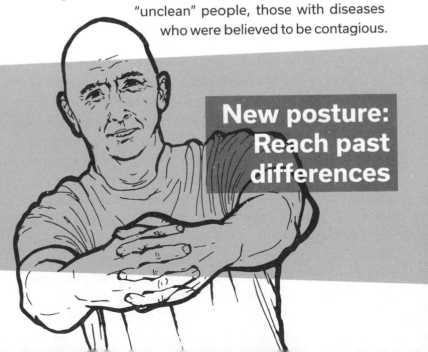

New posture: Reach past differences

He even engaged with Roman soldiers, despised foreign oppressors. In a culture where women were devalued, he treated them with respect and equality. They were among his closest associates. While traveling, his disciples were shocked to find him speaking to a mixed-race female Samaritan, a group most Jews detested. When his disciples argued about which of them was the greatest, he said, "Be at peace with each other."

Learning to Make Peace and Reach Past Differences

What practices might help us move from dividing to embracing one another?

Reach out to reconnect and realign. The place to begin peacemaking is in our closest relationships. Jesus said, "If . . . your brother or sister has something against you, [drop what you are doing]. . . . [G]o and be reconciled to them." How do I know if I need to make peace? One familiar sign is what I like to call the *ugh* in my stomach. When a certain person walks into the room or their name comes up in a conversation, I instantly feel a tightening in my stomach. Some people feel this in their head or chest. Our bodies alert us to relational tensions. If we ignore these signals, it can lead to further conflict and potential violence. When you sense tension in a relationship but aren't sure why, you can always ask, "Are we okay? Did I do something to offend you?"

In Ninefold Path groups we encourage each other to take steps toward interpersonal reconciliation. I invite people to write down the names of anyone who gives them the *ugh* in their stomach. There are a variety of reasons why someone might give you the *ugh*. You might have lost touch, and the distance makes you feel insecure. When my friend Dave moved away, we gradually grew apart. Whenever I thought of him, I would get the *ugh* in my stomach. I wondered if I'd done something to offend him. When this happens, we can reach out to reconnect. I texted Dave and said, "Hey, I was just thinking of you. I'm sorry we've lost touch. I want you to know I'm grateful for the time we walked close together." He quickly texted me back, "I'm also grateful for you, buddy. Hope you are doing well." Immediately, I felt the *ugh* go away.

Another cause of the *ugh* can be a disappointment or unmet expectations. When I saw my friend Richard, I felt the *ugh* and suddenly remembered he had called me two months before to see if we could have lunch. I was busy at the time and never called him back. I think it is reasonable to expect a return call. I quickly apologized and set up a time to meet and the *ugh* went away.

Sometimes tension develops because of differing expectations or unclear agreements. I once mentored someone who hoped we would become work associates. I never promised this, and it wasn't a good fit. Nevertheless, they became resentful and our relationship became tense. Gently, I had to initiate a clarifying conversation. I empathized with their disappointment, and we explored the differences in our understanding. At other times I've put expectations on people they never agreed to and have had to realign and readjust my outlook.

Reach past differences to reconcile with those you have wronged. Sometimes we feel the *ugh* because we know we've broken a promise or wronged another person. In this case we are invited to make peace by seeking forgiveness and making amends.

When my friend Stian, a Norwegian, was asked about who gave him the *ugh* in his stomach, he shared this story:

> I can only think of one person I've wronged that I haven't made peace with, but it was so long ago. When I was fourteen, I stole a classmate's bicycle. He had moved to my town as a refugee from Vietnam. I took the parts I wanted off his bike and threw the frame into the woods. I didn't think much about it, but three years later I went with my church to do door-to-door witnessing. Guess whose house I ended up at? Suddenly I found myself face-to-face with the one whose bike I'd stolen. I felt like a total fake. What I really wanted to share I kept to myself. Years went by. I would think about what I'd done and feel ashamed. At church meetings I would go up to the altar for prayer. People assured me that

God had forgiven me. It felt like a huge relief to let the tears roll while people laid hands on me, but the results were always temporary. The boy and the bike kept haunting me. I still think about it to this day, but I'm not sure what I could do to make peace after all these years. I don't even remember his name.

Rachael, another member of our group said, "Stian, you have to reconcile with this guy! Have you ever tried to contact him and make things right? These days, with the internet, it's not hard to find someone."

Stian reached out to an old friend on social media and got a phone number. He texted and said, "Hello Anton. I am the one who stole your bike twenty years ago. Can we talk?" When they met for tea, Anton forgave him immediately. But Stian felt like there was something yet to be done. *I have to offer him my racing bike*, he thought. It was an old classic he had been working on throughout the winter. Stian asked Anton, "Do you have a bicycle?" Anton said, "The only bike I ever owned was the one you stole from me." Anton accepted the bike as compensation. Reflecting later, Stian said, "I watched him pedal away and the burden I carried for two decades was no more." Stian had done what was necessary for reconciliation to occur, and the circle was now complete.

PRACTICE *Take inventory of your relationships.* Who gives you the *ugh* in your stomach? Is there anyone that you need to make peace with right now?

Steps to Reconciliation

"If it is possible, as far as it depends on you, live at peace with everyone."

- If it is safe for the other person, approach and admit where you were wrong. If you aren't sure what the issue is, check in to see if there is an offense.

- Listen openly to the person's experience of your behavior. Reflect on what you hear: "I hear you saying that it hurt you when I . . ."

- Consider what you are willing to own and admit what you can. Use statements like, "I was wrong. I am sorry I hurt you. Will you please forgive me?"

- Make amends. If you are not sure what would be appropriate, ask.

- Explain the pressures or disordered thinking that led you to hurt them. Knowing this might make it easier for them to forgive you. But be clear you are not making an excuse for what you did.

Reach out to cross boundaries to connect. In your community what kinds of people are typically left out or treated with disdain? In many places it's refugees, undocumented immigrants, those without housing, people with disabilities or mental health conditions, older people, and minority ethnic or religious groups.

In the United States many people are suspicious of those with a Muslim heritage. A few years ago I was invited to participate in a friendship day at a local masjid (mosque). When my friend Joanna and I arrived, Zaahid met us at the door. He directed Joanna to the women's section and showed me how to perform *wudu*, the ritual washing. Then we went in to pray. That was the beginning of my friendship with the sheikh and members of the masjid. A few months later they invited some of my friends and me to the Eid al-Fitr feast at the end of Ramadan. We were treated like honored guests and given mounds of delicious food. We talked with people from many different countries and discovered how much we have in common living as devout people in a largely secular city.

Later, Joanna and I organized a group of Jews and Christians to visit the masjid for another friendship day. The sheikh's son-in-law and daughters shared about their Islamic heritage. The sheikh said, "Our masjid attracts Muslims from all over the world. They each come with ideas about what Islam is, like how you must eat or dress when you pray. I tell them, 'That is your culture, it is not Islam.' The same is true of all of us here. Ninety-five percent of what Jews, Christians, and Muslims believe is the same. Why do we choose to focus on our differences instead of what we have in common?"

Not long after this, President Donald Trump declared a ban on travel from seven Islamic countries. This would prevent my friends from visiting their wives and children back home. I knew how upsetting this would be, so I stopped in to Friday prayer. After the sheikh's sermon, he said, "Brother Mark, would you like to say a few words?" He invited me to the front and handed me the microphone. I told them I was sad about the travel ban. "You don't need me to tell you this, but you have as much right to be here as anyone. With God's help we will get through this time. We are in this together." Dozens of men lined up to shake my hand, and the younger men asked to have their pictures taken with me.

Later the sheikh took me aside and said, "In the days of the Prophet Muhammad, when the Christians traveled through Mecca, the prophet said, 'We must provide a place for them to worship in the mosque.'" This was his way of telling me, "You are welcome to pray with us in your own way." Imagine how different Muslim-Christian relations would be if Christians invited Muslims to pray and eat in their churches!

In my crosscultural friendships there are times when I've tried to represent all Americans, all Christians, or all White people. It's a lot of pressure to represent millions of people, an entire nation, or an entire religion. Conversations are polite but rarely go deeper. In my experience it works better to speak without labels, heart-to-heart, and focus on the hopes, joys, questions, and sorrows we share in common.

Reach out to avoid us-versus-them language. Peacemaking is hard because the differences are real. When we encounter differences, the easiest thing is to caricature the other person's perspective, withdraw from them, or simply keep pushing our views. The media industry knows that the best way to attract clicks, eyeballs, and revenue is to stoke conflict, alarm, and controversy. If you want to see how pervasive this mentality is, trying going a day or a week without using language that labels, stereotypes, and divides (for example, *liberal*, *conservative*, *Christian*, *atheist*, *capitalist*, *socialist*). See how it shapes your heart and interactions in new ways.

If you are part of an excluded minority group, how can you be a peacemaker? Just showing up in majority culture spaces can be a courageous act. I spoke about peacemaking at a church and mentioned that many religious communities use othering language to talk about gay, trans, and nonbinary people. I mentioned the statistical likelihood that four or five people in the room identify as LGBTQ. Imagine how this stigmatizing language makes those people feel! For this reason many people keep their identity a secret or simply leave their religious communities. Afterward, a person approached me and said, "You were talking about me and my partner. I know many people here don't understand our identity or support our choices. But we are here anyway because our faith is important to us. We want to belong and we need the support of this community."

✝ ✝ ✝

How do we keep our differences from becoming toxic? We are invited to give up the need to win and to be right, to step out of our echo chambers. It takes tenacity to stay engaged across differences, to focus on commonalities, to be humble and curious, to listen, to seek to understand another's experience, perspective, and animating desires. Where there is difference or conflict, someone has to go first, having the courage to initiate contact and seek peace. This Beatitude invites us to move from dividing to embracing: *Blessed are the peacemakers, for they will be called children of God.*

May we listen, reach past our differences, embrace one another as family, and follow the way of peacemaking.

8

The Way of Surrender

Embrace Suffering, Keep Doing Good

Blessed are those who are [mistreated for doing good], for theirs is the kingdom of heaven.

MATTHEW 5:10

One evening Lisa and I were walking through downtown Wichita. When the light turned green, we stepped into the crosswalk. To our left, music blasted from a vintage muscle car stopped at the intersection. As we passed, the car revved its engine and suddenly lurched forward nearly hitting us! Startled, I jumped back and pulled Lisa to safety. My heart pounded. When I looked back, I saw the driver pointing at us and laughing! He had let the car jerk forward on purpose just to scare us! Curse words ran through my mind. I wanted to scream and throw a rock through his windshield.

? ▪ What about you? When you are treated unjustly, how do you tend to react?

When we are mistreated, our first instinct is to react defensively. We want to get even, punishing the person who acted so unjustly. The position that embodies this is the 1930s Hollywood movie character with raised fists who says, "Oh yeah, wise guy, you want a piece of me?" We don't always have the courage to fight back directly. We may turn away to vent our frustrations to others: "Can you believe what that guy in the car did to me?" We go sideways with our pain hoping others will agree and take up our offense. This impulse is responsible for so many group splits and family dramas.

Much of the time it feels good to do good. We are often rewarded for being kind. You greet someone, and they greet you back. You step in to help someone, and they say thank you. You give love and receive love. But what about those times when doing the right thing or simply minding your own business leads to pain? You treat someone kindly, and they are rude in return. You blow the whistle at work, and it costs you a promotion—or even your job. You speak up for a mistreated person or group and lose your reputation and friendships.

When we are mistreated, it can feel like we've been singled out. You wonder, *What did I do to deserve this?* Pain is an inevitable result of human freedom. When we choose to do good, we and others benefit. When we choose to do wrong, we and others suffer.

Though we all struggle to navigate these difficulties, some of us, based on personality, are especially prone to being paralyzed by the resistance we face. Sad and angry feelings overwhelm us. Injustice stops us in our tracks. Will we let resistance and difficulty define us, or will we gain the resiliency and perspective to keep moving forward?

A well-known fable is often portrayed in children's cartoons. One day a man goes to work and is berated by his boss. He arrives home fuming and upbraids his wife.

First instinct: React defensively

She slams the door and runs from the house in tears. In the yard she harshly scolds her daughter who had been innocently playing. The girl takes out her anger on her younger brother by pinching him until he screams. Furious, the boy kicks the family dog. The dog chases and catches the family cat, biting it. The cat screeches and then hunts down a mouse, clawing its tail. Round and round it goes. The message is simple. When we are treated unjustly, we often transmit our pain to others. Evil perpetuates evil until someone dares to break the cycle.

What if we could learn to process pain without transmitting it to others? What if we could find the resilience to keep doing good, no matter what resistance we face? What would that be like? Would you like to find a new way to respond to being treated unfairly?

In the teaching on the hill Jesus said, "Blessed are those who are [mistreated for doing good], for theirs is the kingdom of heaven." Jesus demonstrated a radical alternative to our typical responses to being treated unjustly. When religious leaders viciously attacked his reputation, he answered calmly. When he was betrayed by his closest friend and turned over to the authorities, he quietly surrendered to arrest. When falsely accused and put on trial, he did not defend himself but remained silent.

The Posture of Nonviolent Resistance

We've come to the most counterintuitive and counter-cultural teachings of Jesus. He instructed his disciples to do what he modeled,

> You have heard that it was said, "Eye for eye, and tooth for tooth." But I tell you, do not resist an evil person. If anyone slaps you on the right cheek, turn to them the other cheek also. And if anyone wants to sue you and take your shirt, hand over your coat as well. If anyone forces you to go one mile, go with them two miles. Give to the one who asks you, and do not turn away from the one who wants to borrow from you.

Jesus gave these instructions when Israel was under Roman occupation. A Roman soldier could come into a person's house and demand that they cook them a meal. A soldier could stop someone on the road and force them to carry their heavy pack the legally mandated distance of a mile. Instead of resisting or retaliating, Jesus invites us to choose nonviolence: to offer what is demanded of us and more. We are invited to take on a posture of nonviolent resistance. Imagine lowering and crossing your arms, as you would when giving yourself up to be arrested and handcuffed.

New posture:
Nonviolent
resistance

Learning to Embrace Suffering and Keep Doing Good

What practices might help us move from resistance to resiliency?

Keep doing good by choosing nonviolence. Those of us who are survivors of domestic violence or racial prejudice may find the invitation to surrender particularly challenging or problematic. It could sound like I'm saying, "Let people walk all over you" or "Stay in an abusive situation." Here the ordering of the Beatitudes is important. What if the Beatitudes map a progressive journey of spiritual development? First, trust the Creator's care. Then, lament what is broken and wait for divine comfort. Affirm your inherent dignity and worth. Embrace your agency and power. Receive mercy and respond with compassion. Tell the truth and live wholeheartedly. Reach past differences to find common ground. And then surrender to suffering. The order is important. Only after you can affirm these realities can you confidently resist evil through nonviolence. The surrender response must come from a place of strength, confidence, and courage.

What is the deeper reality that can empower us to bless those who mistreat us? We are part of the cosmic struggle between good and evil. When we are mistreated and act combatively, we perpetuate the evil that is in the world. When we respond with nonviolence, we break the cycle. Love is stronger than hate, and no pain is final.

One night my neighbors Jose and Gabriella were awakened by the sound of a burglar crawling through the window into their bedroom. Jose resisted the urge to act aggressively. Instead, he calmly said, "Sir, you need to leave now." The man obediently crawled back out the window. When the police arrived later, they told Gabriella, "Your husband's choice to de-escalate the situation likely saved both of your lives."

When someone approaches us aggressively, we tend to match their energy, which usually escalates the tension. If we have the foresight to respond calmly, we can take the charge out of the interaction and give space for creative solutions. Nonviolence can be a tricky and complex skill to apply. My friend Helen has an adolescent son on the autism spectrum. He lashes out with angry words and sometimes physical aggression. It's very challenging not to match the volume and negative energy he directs toward her. With practice she has learned to subvert what comes at her. When he yells, she speaks calmly, letting him know the boundaries: "I ask that you treat me with respect. I am leaving the room until you can calm down." It doesn't always work, but at least she is able to maintain calm control in what sometimes feels like an impossible situation.

Keep doing good by praying for your enemies. Our normal pattern is to love the people who love us and despise the people who treat us badly. Jesus invites us into a new way: "Love your enemies, do good to those who hate you, bless those who curse you, pray for those who mistreat you." You may hesitate to say you have enemies. But an enemy is simply anyone who is hostile to you or threatens your well-being. It might also be a person who has demonstrated prejudice toward you or a public figure who expresses opposition or disdain toward the most vulnerable. Given this definition, who would you consider to be your enemies?

At one of my first jobs as a groundskeeper, my foreman disliked me. He spoke harshly, ordered me around, and gave me the most difficult jobs. At breaks in the mechanic shop he wouldn't even acknowledge my presence. I certainly considered him to be an enemy. I decided to try out Jesus' instruction to "pray for those who mistreat you." Over the next couple of weeks his demeanor toward me dramatically changed. We even became friends. I don't think it was necessarily anything mystical or supernatural. Praying for him every day changed my attitude, which shifted the energy between us.

When I'm struggling to love someone who has hurt me, I find a picture of them and look at it each morning while speaking this blessing:

May you find peace
embrace goodness and love
and experience what is most real and true.

PRACTICE *Pray for your enemies.* Take a moment right now to pray this blessing for someone you consider to be an enemy.

Keep doing good by blessing those who curse you. I regularly travel to Bangladesh to visit friends who are part of the Christian minority there. Bangladesh is 90 percent Muslim, 9 percent Hindu, and less than 1 percent Christian. My friends regularly experience persecution. They are carefully watched by the police and the government. I've been present when they received threatening phone calls. Several of them have spent months in jail. Despite this they smile and are joyfully open with their Muslim and Hindu neighbors.

Once, I was leading a Ninefold Path retreat at an Islamic conference center outside Dhaka. Our meeting room was located just below the mosque. One of my friends said, "Brother Mark, perhaps we should wait to do our team-building games until our Muslim brothers are done praying." His deference impressed me. My friends greet each person they meet according to that person's ethnic and religious identity. When they encounter a Hindu person they say, "*Namaskar.*" When they greet a Muslim they say, "*Assalamu alaikum*." And when they greet a fellow Christian, they say, "*Immanuel*" (God with us). This reminds me of what Jesus said, "If you love those who love you, what reward will you get? . . . And if you greet only your own people, what are you doing more than others? . . . Be perfect, therefore, as your heavenly Father is perfect."

† † †

Jesus' teachings on nonviolence are perhaps the most well-known and least followed of all of his instructions. Historically, they have been applied more outside the Christian church than inside. Since Christianity was legalized under Constantine in AD 313, Christianity has often aligned with systems of power, conquest, and violence. From the Middle Ages through the Enlightenment (eighteenth century), many of the bloodiest wars in Europe were initiated by people who identified as Christians. And many of those wars were waged against other Christians. There are few exceptions of Christian groups that practiced nonviolence.

We are part of broken structures and systems in which institutions are set up to protect the interests of the powerful while others are excluded and oppressed. If you haven't experienced much suffering for doing right, it may be because you've been on the side of power. Love compels us to speak up, to act in the interests of those without power, to meet oppression with creative resistance. When we do this, we join the cosmic struggle between good and evil. We embrace the possibility of suffering as a necessary and inevitable part of living in a divided world. When we choose to love our enemies and bless those who curse us, we cast our vote for goodness and love, and in the end love will win. This Beatitude invites us to move from an instinct of reacting defensively to a posture of nonviolent resistance: *Blessed are those who [are mistreated for doing good], for theirs is the kingdom of heaven.*

May we resist evil, embrace suffering, commit to doing good no matter the cost, and walk in the way of surrender.

9

The Way of Radical Love

Have Hope, Live Fearlessly

*Blessed are you when people insult you, [mistreat]
you and falsely say all kinds of evil against you
because of me. Rejoice and be glad, because great
is your reward in heaven, for in the same way they
[mistreated] the prophets who were before you.*

MATTHEW 5:11-12

Russell was getting older and hadn't been to church for a while when I visited. When I knocked, I heard a large dog barking and clawing at the door. Russell yelled, "I'll be there in a minute." I noticed bars over the windows, which seemed out of place in an upper-class neighborhood like this one. After restraining the dog and unlatching three deadbolt locks, Russell welcomed me in.

The living room was lined with fifty-five-gallon barrels of water kept in case of an earthquake. Conspiracy books were stacked on the stand by his chair. The dining room and kitchen were piled waist deep with bags of canned food and dry goods. Other rooms were stockpiled with power tools, generators, and safety equipment still in their boxes. Later, I learned about the pistol Russell kept under his pillow, his cache of bullets, and thousands of dollars in cash stashed in the clutter. Looking around, it was clear this was the home of someone desperately afraid.

I don't have fears about physical safety like Russell. But I am afraid of what others think of me and let their opinions dictate my sense of worth. I also fixate on money and basic necessities like food, shelter, and clothing. Our fears aren't always rational. If you saw my house, cupboards, and bank accounts, you'd know that I'm not in imminent danger of going hungry.

My friend Christine works as an oncology nurse, helping terminally ill people in the last days and hours of their lives. She says,

> What impresses me is how differently people approach their final moments. From my observation, my clients who have been long-term practitioners of mindfulness seem peaceful and unafraid, accepting death as a necessary passage. They gracefully consent to whatever comes next. What shocks me

is how many of my clients who self-identify as Christians navigate the last moments of their lives. Often, they seem utterly terrified, with family members surrounding them weeping bitterly. This makes no sense to me. We have a faith story that tells us not to fear, that God is here with us, and that after we die we get to spend eternity reunited in paradise.

The critical moments of life reveal where our true hope lies. There can be a disconnect between what we profess to believe and what we show we believe in practice.

> **? What about you? What are you most afraid of? How has fear shaped your life?**

Psychologists and philosophers speculate that fear is a primary motivator of human behavior. Fear for personal safety. Fear of losing control or freedom. Fear of what others think of us. Our first instinct is to be afraid. Ultimately, we fear nonexistence. The physical embodiment of this is crouching low and covering your head in self-protection. When we are afraid, we hold tightly to whatever we believe preserves our survival.

Though we all have fears, some of us, based on personality, are particularly vulnerable. We crave safety and assurance and look to structures and authority figures to provide the certainty we desire. Fear can keep us from doing what is right and standing up to power when it is important to do so. To put it bluntly, fear is what fuels fascist and authoritarian regimes. When we are afraid, we are susceptible to strongman leaders who fan the flames of panic and present themselves as the solution. In Nazi Germany most people supported Adolf Hitler because they craved stability—with catastrophic results! Fear is the opposite of love. Love invites us to be courageous. Fear leads to cowardice.

What if we could learn to live in a new way? What if instead of being afraid, we could face our fears and pursue radical love? How might the world be different if we dared to do good no matter what the cost? Would you like to learn to live and love more courageously?

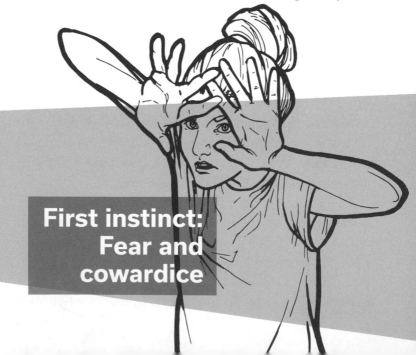

First instinct: Fear and cowardice

In his teaching on the hill, Jesus said, "Blessed are you when people insult you, [mistreat] you and falsely say all kinds of evil against you because of me."

While we all experience suffering, Jesus suggests that particular difficulties will come to those who follow his way of life: a way of trust, lament, humility, justice, compassion, right motive, peacemaking, and surrender. If we had to summarize the path he lived and taught, we could say it was a way of radical love. If we follow love far enough, we will be misunderstood, made fun of, falsely accused, and mistreated. Radical love might cost you your life—as it cost Jesus his life.

The Posture of Radical Love

With the premonition that the authorities were conspiring to have him tortured and executed, Jesus took a few of his disciples with him to a garden to pray. While there he struggled to overcome fear. He agonized over his fate with such intensity that the blood vessels in his forehead burst! What finally allowed Jesus to willingly give himself up to be arrested, tortured, and executed? He had hope that life is eternal and that death is not final.

Imagine holding out your arms in a posture of crucifixion. That's the posture of fearless radical love.

Learning to Have Hope and Live Fearlessly

What practices might help us move from fear to courage?

Live fearlessly by dying to the small, separate self.
Jesus had a strange way of recruiting followers. Essentially, he said, "I'm going to be publicly executed, and you can only be a student of my way if you are ready to suffer and die with me." He invited his disciples to follow his example of self-denial:

> Whoever wants to be my disciple must deny themselves and take up their cross and follow me. For whoever wants to save their life will lose it, but whoever loses their life for me will find it. What good will it be for someone to gain the whole world, yet forfeit their soul? Or what can anyone give in exchange for their soul?

New posture:
Radical love

Jesus presents us with a counterintuitive paradox. Life comes through death. In order to save your life, you have to lose it. Holding on tightly to the small self keeps us from experiencing full contact with reality. It must die so that we can live. The illusion that keeps us from living heroically is that death is the end.

The earliest followers of Jesus took his invitation to self-denial quite literally. Ten out of twelve of his first disciples died as martyrs—they were stabbed, stoned, beaten, or crucified because they believed in Jesus as the living way. When Jesus was killed, his disciples scattered. Days later they were publicly testifying to his resurrection at the risk of imprisonment and death. This dramatic shift in their behavior is often cited by historians as evidence that Jesus did indeed come back to life from the dead. He proved that death is not final. Why else would they suddenly become so bold?

Recognizing that death is inevitable but not final expands our perspective and frees us from desperately clinging to what is impermanent. What will remain after you die? Your soul is the part of you that is connected to the eternal source of life that cannot be destroyed. Death cannot disrupt what is most essential to your well-being. When Jesus tells us to pick up our cross and follow him, he is inviting us to gain a more cosmic and eternal perspective on our existence. Die to the small, separated self that believes what is here now is everything. Die to the constructed ego identity that sees itself as independent from its source. Wake up to the reality of hope in life after life. The most important things last forever.

Paul, an early follower of Jesus, lived and taught death to self. He wrote, "I have been crucified with Christ and I no longer live, but Christ lives in me. The life I now live in the body, I live by faith in the Son of God, who loved me and gave himself for me." In another letter Paul wrote, "I die daily." Each day we have an opportunity to die to the false self and say yes to life, love, and hope.

When we die to the false self, we no longer have anything to be afraid of because we have nothing to protect. John, a close companion of Jesus, wrote, "There is no fear in love. But perfect love drives out fear." This is a safe universe to live in. Nothing can separate you from what is most essential to your well-being. If we continue to be afraid, we have yet to fully encounter transforming love. We are still operating out of the constructed ego that is disconnected from the ultimate reality.

PRACTICE *Risk radical love.* Right now, pause for a moment to reflect on these questions: How would you live if you weren't afraid to die? What is worth giving your life for? What might it look like for you to live fearlessly and love radically?

Live fearlessly by choosing to do good, even when it's costly. Jesus gave his disciples this instruction:

"Love each other as I have loved you. Greater love has no one than this: to lay down one's life for one's friends." Death to the small self frees us to love radically. What is the difference between everyday love and radical love? Everyday love is easy. It's the natural kind of love we have for the people we feel closest to. Like the affection of lovers or close friends, or the love a parent has for their child. Radical love is costly. It often involves suffering. It means doing hard things because they are right and good.

People such as Harriet Tubman, Martin Luther King Jr., and Dietrich Bonhoeffer stand out as heroic icons of doing good no matter what the cost. Throughout history people have endured violence, arrest, imprisonment—and even death—for standing up for what's right. We tend to see these individuals as exceptional examples of goodness and sacrifice. But what if this is a way we're all invited to live?

History shows that if we speak and act in solidarity with those who suffer on the margins, we will also be marginalized. The earliest followers of Jesus understood that following his radical way of love would inevitably lead to resistance and difficulty: "Everyone who wants to live a godly life in Christ Jesus will be persecuted." If we haven't suffered for doing good, what does that suggest about the fear-based choices we've made? Have we put personal comfort above doing what is good and right?

What is the good you hesitate to do because of what it might cost you? Is there an issue, cause, or situation of injustice that you don't speak up about because you fear the loss of reputation or opposition from people who are important to you?

Here are some of the most common responses I hear when I present these questions:

▶ I hesitate to vocalize my concerns about injustice because I know it will offend and create distance from family and friends.

▶ Someone mistreated me. I think it would help them to know how their behavior affects others, but I'm afraid of how they might react.

▶ I hesitate to get closer to someone with high needs because I know loving them will take extra care and time and may complicate my life.

▶ At work I witnessed something unethical. I'm afraid that if I blow the whistle it might cost me a promotion or my job.

▶ I disagree with the policies of a group I'm part of. I have voiced my concerns, but the leaders are unwilling to change. My conscience tells me to withdraw, but that will mean a loss of community and connections.

My friends Tim and Michelle run a business where many of their employees are migrant workers. Tim and Michelle live in an area where most people they know take a hard line on immigration. But Tim and Michelle care about their employees and see how current policies have separated families. They knew that if they were vocal about their concerns, they would be stereotyped and potentially lose many of their friends. Eventually, they decided to advocate for these families anyway. In their context this was a costly choice to love radically.

You may be vulnerable to fear, but that doesn't mean you have to let it drive your life. You can choose to be courageous. Radical love invites us to endure, to keep on doing good, whatever the cost, to believe that right action is more important than any opposition we may face.

Live fearlessly by celebrating that love is greater than fear and death. One of the few rituals Jesus instituted among his disciples was the Lord's Table, eating bread and drinking wine as a celebration of how life comes after death. In a poignant moment during the Passover festival, he took the bread used to commemorate the ancient event and said,

> "Take and eat; this is my body." Then he took a cup, and when he had given thanks, he gave it to them, saying, "Drink from it. . . . This is my blood . . . which is poured out . . . for the forgiveness of sins. I tell

you, I will not drink from this fruit of the vine from now on until that day when I drink it new with you in my Father's kingdom."

Soon after Jesus came back to life, his disciples began commemorating his death and resurrection by repeating this ritual, which they called the Lord's Table. Celebrating the Lord's Table can help you remember the way of radical love. When I eat the bread and drink the wine, I try to keep three things in mind:

- ▶ I am forgiven and not separated from the eternal life of God.

- ▶ I am united in solidarity with everyone on the planet who seeks the way of Jesus.

- ▶ I am invited to die to my small self and say yes to love no matter the cost.

✝ ✝ ✝

When you have something worth dying for that means more to you than any resistance or persecution you might face—that's something to rejoice about. In each moment that we seek radical love, we join the lineage of those who have gone before us, who have lived from the hope that love is greater than fear, and that death is not final. This Beatitude invites us to move from fear to courage: *Blessed are you when people insult you, [mistreat] you and falsely say all kinds of evil against you because of me. Rejoice and be glad, because great is your reward in heaven, for in the same way they [mistreated] the prophets who were before you.*

May we live fearlessly with hope and courage and walk in the way of radical love.

Conclusion

Living the Ninefold Path

One day while working on this project, I went to the pharmacy to pick up a prescription. As I waited, I noticed the person sitting next to me rummaging through a backpack. He suddenly pulled out a pistol, cocked the trigger, and took aim. My mind raced and my heart beat wildly. Is he about to rob the store? Should I tackle him to the floor?

This may sound strange, but I took a deep breath and thought about how the ninefold path might apply to my situation. The way of surrender: *Mark, see if you can find a nonviolent way to de-escalate this situation.* The way of radical love: *Mark, don't be afraid. Life comes after death. Be courageous!*

Other people began to notice the man brandishing the weapon. I had to act quickly. I turned to him and gently said, "Hey friend, what kind of gun is that?" He murmured incoherently. "I can see it is making people around you nervous. If the security guard notices, he might call the police—and you might not make it out of this store without being arrested or shot. I think it would be best if you put the gun away." He slowly lowered the weapon and put it back in his bag.

My name was called. I approached the counter and discretely explained the situation to the pharmacist—suggesting they keep an eye on this person. On my next visit I followed up with the pharmacist. He told me the person left without incident. I like to think that my journey with the ninefold path made a difference.

Most mornings I go for a short walk and use the Beatitudes to set my intentions for the day. I hold each posture, recite the Beatitude, and reflect on a question (see "Ninefold Path Prayer and Examen Questions"). I'm pretty sure some of my neighbors think I'm crazy, especially when I walk around the square doing jazz hands. Each day I have a choice. I can live by my first instincts: anxiety, denial, competition, apathy, contempt, deception, division, anger, and fear, or I can choose to live from a higher state of consciousness: trust, lament, humility, justice, compassion, right motive, peacemaking, surrender, and radical love. If I've been rehearsing jealous thoughts I'm reminded that we all have equal dignity and worth. If I'm frustrated with a coworker I'm reminded to look with eyes of compassion.

I've also seen how the ninefold path can transform group culture. I was traveling with a team leading Ninefold

Path events in East Africa. Long days, hot weather, travel on bumpy roads, and living in close quarters brought out the best and worst in us. The Beatitudes gave us a shared vocabulary for navigating these experiences together. It was heartbreaking to meet malnourished children in rural villages with bloated stomachs—especially when the help we could give was so limited. We made space to mourn. If one of us made a critical statement about another development organization, a fellow team member would gently say, "Friend, you don't have to compare our work to theirs or put them on the other side. Reach past differences. We're all in this together."

During this project, I've been through several unprecedented challenges. The Beatitudes were right there inviting me to face the pain, let go of my resentments, and bless those who mistreated me. I'm reminded that the ninefold path of Jesus doesn't promise an escape from what's hard in life. But it does provide a way to navigate our difficulties with courage, comfort, and resiliency.

Mahatma Gandhi carefully studied Jesus' teachings on the hill: "Do not resist an evil person. If anyone slaps you on the right cheek, turn to them the other cheek also." They inspired his idea of *satyagraha* or nonviolent resistance. Martin Luther King Jr. later applied Gandhi's method as a weapon in the struggle for civil rights and racial equality in the United States. King said that his use of nonviolence was inspired by reading a book about

Gandhi by E. Stanley Jones, an American missionary and friend of Gandhi. In a small book on the teachings of Jesus, Jones reflected,

> A little man in a loin cloth in India picks out from the Sermon on the Mount one of its central principles, applies it as a method for gaining human freedom, and the world, challenged and charmed, bends over to catch the significance of the great sight. It is a portent of what would happen if we would take the whole of the Sermon on the Mount and apply it to the whole of life. It would renew our Christianity— it would renew the world.

I hope that this book has inspired you to consider how your life can be changed and how the world can be transformed if we truly make the ninefold path of Jesus our guide for life. Let's return to what is most real and true.

> May we learn to
> live with open hands
> mourn what's broken
> serve with self-respect
> use our power for good
> look with compassion
> walk in honesty
> reach past differences
> suffer for love
> and live fearlessly, following the way of
> radical love.

Acknowledgments

This book would not have been possible without the support of Lifewords (lifewords.global) and NINE BEATS Collective (9beats.org). Thank you to Steve Bassett and Danielle Welch for inviting me to collaborate on this project. Rozella Haydée White, Christine Suh, Eric Leroy Wilson, and Matt Valler were part of the "hothouse" conversations in Malibu that shaped my understanding of how the Beatitudes speak to contemporary life. Further refinements of language and approach were worked out with some of us in London, with the addition of Dan Hardie. Danielle Welch worked closely with me to develop and edit *The Ninefold Path Notebook* and *Learning Lab Guide* from which this book was developed. Much of the content in this book is credited to her keen mind, ear for language, and the hundreds of hours we spent discussing and refining this material together.

Thank you to the individuals who helped us pilot early iterations of this material: Lisa Scandrette, David Kludt,

Richard Lundblad, Jason Royce, Anna Freij, Alex Drew, Aaron Niequist, and Jason Feffer.

Thank you to the individuals and groups who provided a platform for us to experiment with this material in contexts around the world: Greenbelt Festival, Church Mission Society, Youthscape, Souster Youth Trust, Bay Area Rescue Mission, Oasis Church London, Newbigin Center (Birmingham), The Practice at Willow Creek, Doing Life Together, South Australian Uniting Aboriginal Islander Christian Congress, Lifewords Nairobi, Live Connection, Compassion International, Bangladesh Nazarene Mission, Micah Network, Formation Experience, Fresh Hope New South Wales, Salvation Army (UK and AU), Vote Common Good, Surrender Festival, and Scripture Union Victoria.

Thank you to the Ninefold Path Lab team at Lifewords: Matt Currey and Cornelia Gaie.

Conversations with Dr. Adam Ghali refined my understanding of the psychological dimensions of the Beatitudes. Jarrod Shappell provided feedback on this manuscript.

Thanks to the team at InterVarsity Press, especially Cindy Bunch, Andrew Bronson, and Lori Neff. And thanks to my agent, Greg Daniel, of Daniel Literary Group.

Thank you to everyone who gave me permission to share your stories!

I am particularly grateful for the partnership and support of my wife, Lisa, who has been my steadfast companion on the journey of the ninefold path.

Ninefold Path Prayer and Examen Questions

"Blessed are the poor in spirit, for theirs is the kingdom of heaven." (Open hands)
What am I most grateful for right now? What do I need and want today?
Lord, lead me in the way of trust.

"Blessed are those who mourn, for they will be comforted." (Head in hands)
What am I sad or disturbed about today? How am I running from pain?
Lord, lead me in the way of lament.

"Blessed are the meek, for they will inherit the earth." (Bow with hand on heart)
What is most true about me? How I can serve and affirm the dignity of others?
Lord, lead me in the way of humility.

"Blessed are those who hunger and thirst [for justice],
for they [will] be satisfied." (Hands crossed over chest)
*Where do I ache for change? How can I use my power
for good?*
Lord, lead me in the way of justice.

"Blessed are the merciful, for they will be shown mercy."
(Make heart with hands)
*For what in my life do I need mercy? Who needs my
mercy and forgiveness?*
Lord, lead me in the way of compassion.

"Blessed are the pure in heart, for they will see God."
(Jazz hands)
*How am I hiding? How can I be more truthful
and wholehearted?*
Lord, lead me in the way of right motive.

"Blessed are the peacemakers, for they will be
called children of God." (Reach out and clasp
hands together)
*Who have I put on the other side of us versus them?
How can I reach past differences?*
Lord, lead me in the way of peacemaking.

"Blessed are those who are [mistreated for doing good], for theirs is the kingdom of heaven." (Hands lowered and crossed)
What is the good I hesitate to do? What is the suffering I need to embrace?
Lord, lead me in the way of surrender.

"Blessed are you when people insult you, [mistreat] you and falsely say all kinds of evil against you because of me. Rejoice and be glad, because great is your reward in heaven, for in the same way they [mistreated] the prophets who were before you." (Arms stretched in posture of a crucifixion)
How can I die to self and lay down my life for others? How can I choose love over fear?
Lord, lead me in the way of radical love.

Summary of the Ninefold Path

The Way of Trust

From anxiety to trust. "Blessed are the poor." We are naturally anxious about survival and having enough. The fight-or-flight response is designed to alert us to danger and move us away from potential threats. This often leads to anxiety, greediness, and striving. To fully thrive we are invited to move from closed-handed anxiety to openhanded trust.

First instinct. Anxiety and worry. Closed hands, tightly grasping and grabbing.

Reality. Divine care and presence. The universe is abundant and we are interdependent. Nothing can separate us from what is most essential to our well-being.

New posture. Open hands

Practices. Open your hands to

- ▶ receive the good
- ▶ share what you have
- ▶ express your desires
- ▶ let go of expectations

The Way of Lament

From avoiding to facing pain. "Blessed are those who mourn." We are naturally pain-avoidant and can easily become compulsive about escaping pain and denying responsibility. To experience true comfort, we are invited to face our pain and wait for comfort.

First instinct. We turn away from pain. Holding hands up to block out whatever we find too difficult to face.

Reality. The comfort of divine presence can meet us in the pain and loneliness of our lives.

New posture. Face pain with lowered chin and head in hands.

Practices. Face pain by

- ▶ making space to mourn (limiting or fasting from distractions)
- ▶ waiting in stillness

- ▶ writing a complaint
- ▶ mourning with those who mourn

The Way of Humility

From competition and comparison to true worth. "Blessed are the meek." We naturally compare ourselves to one another, asking, "Who is the strongest, the smartest, and the best?" To develop a secure sense of identity, we are invited to move from competition and comparisons to embrace our true worth, treating each other with mutual respect.

First instinct. Competition and comparisons. Using your hands to measure and compare.

Reality. We are each made in the divine image, endowed with inherent dignity and worth.

New posture. Hand on heart with head bowed to honor the divine image in yourself and others.

Practices. Bow to

- ▶ the sacred source of your life
- ▶ affirm your inherent dignity and worth
- ▶ honor the dignity and worth of others
- ▶ give and receive help

The Way of Justice

From apathy to agency. "Blessed are those who hunger and thirst for [justice]." We naturally feel small and overwhelmed by the challenges of our world. To fully thrive we are invited to embrace our agency and power to do good.

First instinct. Passive indifference. Hands thrown up in resignation.

Reality. We are powerful beings who shape the world through our choices. We are invited to be agents of justice, fulfilling our Creator's dreams.

New posture. Arms raised and crossed, stepping forward into action.

Practices. Step into action by

- ▸ owning your identity as a liberator
- ▸ imagining the world as it could be
- ▸ making small changes
- ▸ joining the struggle for justice

The Way of Compassion

From judgment and contempt to mercy. "Blessed are the merciful." We develop our sense of right and wrong by evaluating our behavior and judging others' actions. To fully thrive we are invited to move from judgment and contempt to compassionate seeing and forgiveness.

First instinct. Judgment, contempt, and resentment. A judging eye and pointing finger.

Reality. Grace. Mercy triumphs over judgment. We are treated better than our actions deserve.

New posture. Look through the shape of a heart with your hands.

Practices. Look with love by

- ▶ seeing with eyes of compassion
- ▶ practicing positive speech
- ▶ letting go of resentments
- ▶ practicing self-compassion

The Way of Right Motive

From hiding to wholehearted authenticity. "Blessed are the pure in heart." We are naturally sensitive to what others think of us, easily feel shame, and hide behind our masks or personas. To thrive in our relationships, we are invited to become more honest and wholehearted.

First instinct. Being divided. Hiding and pretending behind a mask.

Reality. The truth will eventually come out. God sees everything about you and holds that with tenderness.

New posture. Hands spread to show your true face and true heart. Jazz hands!

Practices. Show the real you by

- ▶ telling the truth about yourself
- ▶ being wholehearted in your decisions
- ▶ practicing secrecy
- ▶ allowing God to see what's inside of you

The Way of Peacemaking

From dividing to embracing. "Blessed are the peacemakers." To create a sense of safety and security we instinctually divide the world into *us* and *them*. To fully thrive we are invited to shift to *we* and embrace one another as family.

First instinct. Us versus them. One hand pointing toward self, the other hand held up like a stop sign.

Reality. We are all children of one Creator and part of a larger whole. There are no sides.

New posture. Arms extended to reach past differences and embrace one another.

Practices. Reach out to

- ▶ reconnect and realign
- ▶ reconcile with those you have wronged

- ▶ cross boundaries to connect
- ▶ avoid us-and-them language

The Way of Surrender

From resistance to resiliency. "Blessed are those who are [mistreated for doing good]." When we are treated unjustly, our instinct is to retaliate. To fully thrive we are invited to surrender to suffering and choose nonviolence.

First instinct. Reacting defensively. Raised fists ready to fight.

Reality. Suffering is inevitable but not final. We are part of a larger cosmic struggle between good and evil. Power is made perfect in weakness.

New posture. Hands lowered and crossed as if presenting yourself to be arrested and handcuffed.

Practices. Keep doing good by

- ▶ choosing nonviolence
- ▶ praying for your enemies
- ▶ blessing those who curse you

The Way of Radical Love

From fear to courage. "Blessed are you when people insult you, [mistreat] you and say all kinds of evil against you because of me." We naturally want to stay alive. Fear makes us self-protective and cowardly. To fully thrive we are invited to overcome fear, die to self, and learn to love courageously.

First instinct. Fear and self-protection. Crouching low and covering your head.

Reality. We are eternal beings connected to the ultimate source of life. Life comes after life, and death is not final.

New posture. Arms stretched out for crucifixion.

Practices. Live fearlessly by

- ▸ dying to your small, separate self
- ▸ choosing to do good even when it's costly
- ▸ celebrating that love is greater than fear and death

Appendix 3

The Beatitudes and Personality

The Beatitudes name nine universal struggles of the human condition. The ninefold path points us back to reality, toward what is most real and true. Perhaps you've felt drawn to certain Beatitudes and more challenged by others. Personality is a likely factor. Some readers may be familiar with the Enneagram personality typology. I believe there is a correlation between the first instincts of the ninefold path and the internal messages of the nine Enneagram types. While it is beyond the scope of this book to explore all the details and nuances of these connections, I offer tentative suggestions for how the Beatitudes speak life into particular personality types. For each Enneagram type I've listed a key Beatitude invitation that counters a core tendency for that type. You may also want to pay particular attention to the key Beatitude invitations related to the stress and growth number dynamics for your type and your wing.

Your personal growth may be accelerated by paying particular attention to these Beatitude invitations.

Type 1: Perfectionist/Reformer

First instinct. Judgment, pointing finger, and judging eye.

Key Beatitude invitation. The way of compassion. Mercy triumphs over judgment, promising kindness that goes beyond the consequences of our actions or the retribution we feel might be deserved.

Stress and growth points. (4) The way of surrender and (7) the way of lament.

Wings. (9) The way of justice or (2) the way of humility.

Type 2: Helper

First instinct. Making comparisons and measuring who is greater than and less than.

Key Beatitude invitation. The way of humility. Embrace the reality that you are beloved not because of what you do for others but for your inherent dignity and worth.

Stress and growth points. (8) The way of trust and (4) the way of surrender.

Wings. (1) The way of compassion or (3) the way of right motive.

Type 3: The Achiever/ Performer

First instinct. Hiding behind a mask or persona.

Key Beatitude invitation. The way of right motive. Step into the light, tell the truth about yourself, and allow God and others to see and love you for who you really are.

Stress and growth points. (9) The way of justice and (6) the way of radical love.

Wings. (2) The way of humility or (4) the way of surrender.

Type 4: The Individualist

First instinct. Reacting with fists up to suffering and injustice.

Key Beatitude invitation. The way of surrender. Embrace suffering as part of a larger cosmic struggle. Develop resilience.

Stress and growth points. (2) The way of humility and (1) the way of compassion.

Wings. (3) The Way of Right Motive or (5) the way of peacemaking.

Type 5: The Investigator/Observer

First instinct. Hand out like a stop sign to define us and them. Me against everyone. My time. My space. My knowledge. My possessions.

Key Beatitude invitation. The way of peacemaking. You are part of a larger whole. Energy is renewable, so it's safe to reach out, give to others, and fully show up.

Stress and growth points. (7) The way of lament and (8) the way of trust.

Wings. (4) The way of surrender or (6) the way of radical love.

Type 6: The Loyalist

First instinct. Cowering in fear and self-protection.

Key Beatitude invitation. The way of radical love. Face your fears. Life comes after life. Die to your small, separate self. Love courageously.

Stress and growth points. (3) The way of right motive and (9) the way of justice.

Wings. (5) The way of peacemaking or (7) the way of lament.

Type 7: The Enthusiast

First instinct. Numbing out and turning away to avoid pain.

Key Beatitude invitation. The way of lament. Stop running from pain; believe that a true source of comfort is near.

Stress and growth points. (1) The way of compassion and (5) the way of peacemaking.

Wings. (6) The way of radical love or (8) the way of trust.

Type 8: The Leader/Challenger

First instinct. Clinched fists grabbing after what is lacking.

Key Beatitude invitation. The way of trust. You don't have to make it on your own. You can be vulnerable and depend on others. We have an abundant provider.

Stress and growth points. (5) The way of peacemaking and (2) the way of humility.

Wings. (7) The way of lament or (9) the way of radical love.

Type 9: The Peacemaker

First instinct. A sense of futility with arms thrown up in resignation.

Key Beatitude invitation. The way of justice. You are not helpless or hopeless. You are a powerful being who shapes the world by your choices. Step into action.

Stress and growth points. (6) The way of radical love and (3) the way of right motive.

Wings. (8) The way of trust or (1) the way of compassion.

Notes

Introduction

4 *a project based on the Beatitudes*: A description of the NINE BEATS Collective can be found at the website 9beats.org.

5 *The Ninefold Path Learning Lab:* Much of the content of this book is based on resources that can be accessed at www.ninefoldpath.org.

8 *We instinctually distrust people*: Bobby Azarian, "Understanding the Racist Brain," *Psychology Today*, September 24, 2018, www.psychologytoday.com/us/blog/mind-in-the-machine/201809/understanding-the-racist-brain.

11 *consider which Beatitude realities you find*: If you are familiar with the Enneagram personality typology, you may notice some connections. See Don Richard Riso and Russ Hudson, *The Wisdom of the Enneagram: The Complete Guide to Psychological and Spiritual Growth for the Nine Personality Types* (New York: Bantam Books, 1999).

1. The Way of Trust

14 *Blessed are you who are poor*: Luke 6:20.

15 *control-oriented personalities*: The way of trust offers a critical invitation to those who identify as Enneagram Eights. See Don Richard Riso and Russ Hudson, *The*

Wisdom of the Enneagram: The Complete Guide to Psychological and Spiritual Growth for the Nine Personality Types (New York: Bantam Books, 1999).

18   *Who of you by worrying*: Luke 12:25.

19   *Do not worry about your life*: Matthew 6:25.

    Do not be anxious about anything: Philippians 4:6.

    [Adonai] is my shepherd: Psalm 23:1.

21   *Give thanks in all circumstances*: 1 Thessalonians 5:18.

22   *Sell your possessions*: Luke 12:33.

    They sold property and possessions: Acts 2:45.

    It is more blessed to give: Acts 20:35.

23   *What do you want me to do*: Mark 10:51.

    Ask and it will be given to you: Matthew 7:7-8.

2. The Way of Lament

30   *personality traits sensitive to pain:* The way of lament offers a critical invitation to those who identify as Enneagram Sevens. See Don Richard Riso and Russ Hudson, *The Wisdom of the Enneagram: The Complete Guide to Spiritual Growth for the Nine Personality Types* (New York: Bantam Books, 1999).

33   *Each heart knows its own bitterness*: Proverbs 14:10.

    Why, my soul, are you downcast?: Psalm 42:5.

36   *Be still, and know that I am God*: Psalm 46:10.

    All shall be well: Julian of Norwich, "The Thirteenth Revelation" in *Revelations of Divine Love*, trans. Clifton Wolters (New York: Penguin, 1966), chap. 27.

    I have stilled and quieted my soul: Psalm 131:2 ASV.

37   *Awake, Lord! Why do you sleep?*: Psalm 44:23-24.

     My God, my God: Psalm 22:1.

39   *mourn with those who mourn*: Romans 12:15.

3. The Way of Humility

43   *Social comparison theory explains*: Several phrases and sentences in this chapter overlap with the author's post, "The Way of Humility," Mark Scandrette, April 24, 2018, www.markscandrette.com/journal.

     The reward center of their brains: Jonathan Dvash, et al., "The Envious Brain: The Neural Basis of Social Comparison," *Human Brain Mapping* 31, no. 11 (November 2010): 1746, https://doi.org/10.1002/hbm.20972.

     When details were added: Hidehiko Takahashi, et al., "When Your Gain Is My Pain and Your Pain Is My Gain: Neural Correlates of Envy and Schadenfreude," *Science* 323, no. 5916 (February 13, 2009): 937-39.

46   *Data suggest that inequality*: Richard Wilkinson and Kate Pickett, *The Spirit Level: Why Greater Equality Makes Societies Stronger*, rev. ed. (New York: Bloomsbury Press, 2011).

     All toil and all achievement: Ecclesiastes 4:4.

47   *fearfully and wonderfully made*: Psalm 139:14.

     There is a story about Jesus: John 13:1-17.

48   *The greatest among you*: Luke 22:26-27.

50   *Thank you for joining me today*: See Denise Mary Champion with Rosemary Dewerse, *Yarta Wandatha* (n.p.: Denise Champion, 2014).

52   *You also should wash*: John 13:14-15.

53   *have formed our personalities*: The way of humility offers a critical invitation to those who identify as Enneagram Twos. See Don Richard Riso and Russ Hudson, *The Wisdom of the Enneagram: The Complete Guide to Psychological and Spiritual Growth for the Nine Personality Types* (New York: Bantam Books, 1999).

55   *Take the lowest place*: Luke 14:10-11.

4. The Way of Justice

57   *While all of us struggle with apathy*: The way of justice offers a critical invitation to those who identify as Enneagram Nines. See Don Richard Riso and Russ Hudson, *The Wisdom of the Enneagram: The Complete Guide to Psychological and Spiritual Growth for the Nine Personality Types* (New York: Bantam Books, 1999).

59   *You are the light of the world*: Matthew 5:14, 16.

   The Spirit of the Lord is on me: Luke 4:18-20.

60   *The kingdom of heaven has come near*: Matthew 4:17.

   The Kingdom of God is within you: Luke 17:21 GNT.

   Seek first the kingdom of God: Matthew 6:33 ESV.

62   *Do unto others what you would:* Matthew 7:12

64   *Learn to do right; seek justice*: Isaiah 1:17.

68   *If anyone, then, knows the good*: James 4:17.

5. The Way of Compassion

70   *Eye for eye*: Leviticus 24:20

   perfectionistic personality tendencies: The way of compassion offers a critical invitation to those who identify as Enneagram Ones. See Don Richard Riso and Russ Hudson, *The Wisdom of the Enneagram : The Complete*

Guide to Psychological and Spiritual Growth for the Nine Personality Types (New York: Bantam Books, 1999).

"the Headcrusher": Headcrusher, played by Mark McKinney on *The Kids in the Hall* (TV series).

73   *Do not judge*: Matthew 7:1-2.

74   *Let any one of you*: John 8:7.

    The LORD is compassionate and gracious: Psalm 103:8, 13.

75   *When he saw the crowds*: Matthew 9:36.

    Jesus looked at him: Mark 10:21.

    When the Lord saw her: Luke 7:13.

78   *What are signs that you*: A version of this section was published in *Conversations Journal* 13, no. 1 (2015).

80   *Research suggests that people*: "Forgiveness: Your Health Depends on It," *Johns Hopkins Medicine*, accessed November 12, 2020, www.hopkinsmedicine .org/health/wellness-and-prevention/forgiveness-your -health-depends-on-it.

81   *Father, forgive them:* Luke 23:34.

    A [person] reaps what [they] sow: Galatians 6:7.

    Forgive us our sins: Luke 11:4.

6. The Way of Right Motive

85   *Where are you?* Genesis 3:9.

    Some of us, based on personality: The way of right motive offers a critical invitation to those who identify as Enneagram Threes. See Don Richard Riso and Russ Hudson, *The Wisdom of the Enneagram : The Complete*

Guide to Psychological and Spiritual Growth for the Nine Personality Types (New York: Bantam Books, 1999).

88   *There is nothing hidden*: Luke 8:17.

Above all else, guard your heart: Proverbs 4:23.

Create in me a clean heart: Psalm 51:10 ESV.

89   *Confess your [mistakes and failures]*: James 5:16.

90   *Let your 'Yes' be 'Yes'*: Matthew 5:37 NKJV.

When you give to the needy: Matthew 6:3.

When you pray: Matthew 6:5.

When you fast: Matthew 6:16-18.

92   *Search me, God*: Psalm 139:23-24.

we live and move: Acts 17:28.

7. The Way of Peacemaking

97   *Some personalities are particularly*: The way of peacemaking offers a critical invitation to those who identify as Enneagram Fives. See Don Richard Riso and Russ Hudson, *The Wisdom of the Enneagram: The Complete Guide to Psychological and Spiritual Growth for the Nine Personality Types* (New York: Bantam Books, 1999).

Our brains are wired to: Bobby Azarian, "Understanding the Racist Brain," *Psychology Today*, September 24, 2018, www.psychologytoday.com/us/blog/mind-in-the-machine/201809/understanding-the-racist-brain.

100   *be at peace with each other*: Mark 9:50.

If . . . your brother or sister: Matthew 5:23-24.

102   *he shared this story*: A version of this story was previously published in Norwegian in *Kunsten å forme livet*

– *plastisk teologi* (in English, *Plastic Theology*) by Stian Kilde Aarebrot (Oslo: Luther forlag, 2018).

104 *If it is possible*: Romans 12:18.

8. The Way of Surrender

111 *Though we all struggle to navigate*: The way of surrender offers a critical invitation to those who identify as Enneagram Fours. See Don Richard Riso and Russ Hudson, *The Wisdom of the Enneagram: The Complete Guide to Psychological and Spiritual Growth for the Nine Personality Types* (New York: Bantam Books, 1999).

113 *You have heard that it was said*: Matthew 5:38-42.

117 *Love your enemies*: Luke 6:27-28.

119 *If you love those who love you*: Matthew 5:46-48.

9. The Way of Radical Love

123 *Though we all have fears*: The way of radical love offers a critical invitation to those who identify as Enneagram Sixes. See Don Richard Riso and Russ Hudson, *The Wisdom of the Enneagram: The Complete Guide to Psychological and Spiritual Growth for the Nine Personality Types* (New York: Bantam Books, 1999).

126 *Whoever wants to be my disciple*: Matthew 16:24-26.

128 *I have been crucified with Christ*: Galatians 2:20.

I die daily: 1 Corinthians 15:31 KJV.

There is no fear in love: 1 John 4:18.

129 *Love each other as I have*: John 15:12-13.

Everyone who wants to live: 2 Timothy 3:12.

131 *Take and eat; this is my body*: Matthew 26:26-29.

Conclusion

136   *Do not resist an evil person*: Matthew 5:39.

137   *A little man in a loincloth*: E. Stanley Jones, *The Christ of the Mount: A Working Philosophy of Life* (New York: The Abingdon Press, 1931), 12-13.

Appendix 3: The Beatitudes and Personality

151   *Some readers may be familiar:* See Don Richard Riso and Russ Hudson, *The Wisdom of the Enneagram: The Complete Guide to Psychological and Spiritual Growth for the Nine Personality Types* (New York: Bantam Books, 1999).

Also by **Mark** and **Lisa Scandrette**

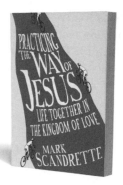

For related products, music, and free videos on each posture, visit www.ninefoldpath.org.

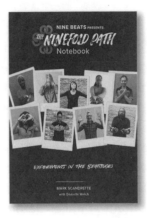

The Ninefold Path Learning Lab written by Mark Scandrette with Danielle Welch, is an eleven-session group journey through the practices mentioned in this book. It includes detailed session outlines, exercises, handouts for homework practices, and links to supplemental videos, music, and other resources. *The Ninefold Path Notebook* (also written by Mark Scandrette with Danielle Welch) is a slim, easy-to-share introduction to the Beatitudes, which can be used with *The Ninefold Path Learning Lab*. This resource is available in packs of five.

For more information on both of these Ninefold Path resources visit www.nine foldpath.org and www.9beats.org. NINE BEATS is an international collective of musicians, troubadours, poets, rebels, provocateurs, teachers, activists, and pilgrims exploring the ancient Bible wisdom known as "The Beatitudes". A double album,"'Nine Beats To The Bar," is also available on all digital platforms.

About the Author

Mark Scandrette is an internationally recognized expert in practical Christian spirituality. He is the executive director of ReImagine, a center for integral Christian practice based in San Francisco. His most recent books include *Free*, *Practicing the Way of Jesus*, *Belonging and Becoming*, and *The Ninefold Path Notebook* and *The Ninefold Path Learning Lab*. In addition to leading retreats and workshops for leaders and teams around the world, Mark teaches in the doctoral program at Fuller Seminary. He is on the creative team for NINE BEATS Collective, an international project exploring the Beatitudes as a twenty-first-century vocabulary for living the way of Jesus. He lives with his family in an old Victorian in San Francisco's Mission District. He loves walking city streets and discovering beauty in unexpected places. He is passionately engaged in sustainability practices and efforts to create flourishing neighborhoods for all people.

For speaking inquiries visit markscandrette.com.